The books of Father Anthony de Mello were written in a multi-religious context to help the followers of other religions, agnostics and atheists in their spiritual search, and they were not intended by the author as manuals of instruction of the Catholic faithful in christian doctrine or dogma.

CALL TO LOVE
Meditations

Anthony de Mello, S.J.

Edited by
James R. Dolan, S.J.

2003
Gujarat Sahitya Prakash
P. Box 70, Anand 388 001,
Gujarat, India

Ist Edition, July 1991
9th Edition, July 2003

ISBN 81 87886 27 7

Price: Rs. 50.00, $ 6.00

Published by: K.T. Mathew, S.J. Gujarat Sahitya Prakash, P.B. 70,
Anand – 388001, Gujarat, India.
Laser set and printed by: S. Abril, S.J., Anand press, P.B. 95,
Gamdi-Anand, Gujarat-388001, India.

CONTENTS

CONTENTS

PRESENTATION

The meditations in this volume are not some new doctrines, nor a book of meditations on christian theology, but the memoirs of a mystic who has had the courage to see reality and therefore was full of compassion and love for all beings and all things, who delighted in everything and in nothing. In a sense, these are autobiographical : they portray the painful route by which Tony was led in the last years of his life to divest himself of all ideologies, to be alone. These deal primarily with the theme of love and obstacles to love : attachments, desires, greed - in one word, conditionings, and how one may be freed from these and come to see, come to love.

These are powerful meditations to help us break out of our prisons of conditioning, free us from our formulae which prevent us from seeing reality. These lead us to realize that in order to reach Truth we need a heart that divests itself of all its programming, all its self interest a heart that has nothing to protect and nothing to ambition for, and hence is fearless and free. These meditations challenge some of the commonly accepted theories life : you can love only when you feel deeply loved by someone etc. They abound in enigmatic statements : you can love only when you are alone, love is, love has no objects etc. Tony helps us to peep into the mystery that is love.

I do no expect all to agree with Tony : many may not want to see what he is pointing at. He was aware that many would prefer their prison walls to the freedom outside; some would want to merely ameliorate their prison conditions. He hoped that a few would have the courage to break out of their prisons and want to see reality and be changed by this seeing. Some would blame him for looking at everything from such a personal angle and for neglecting the social, structural dimensions of reality. He was not blind to these; he was interested rather in presenting a fundamental attitude required in all : social reformers, revolutionaries, christians, hindus, *atheists*— anyone; an attitude like the nishkama karma of the Indian tradition, or what Tony calls the mysticism of non-profit actions, which is necessary in anyone who wants to contribute to the building up of a more just and humane society.

There is, no doubt, a certain amount of repetition; but without sacrificing some of his precious insights, the repetitions could not be avoided.

Joseph Mattam, S.J.

Ahmedabad 7th February 1994

PREFACE

Tony de Mello, along with Dic McHugh and Joe Aizpun presented the classes and directed the therapy at the Sadhana Institute in Lonavla. I was privileged to have the opportunity to visit India and to take part in the 1985-86 Maxi Program. We had group sessions five hours a day, five days each week. While everyone looked forward to the stimulating exchanges and discoveries of class, the highlight of the day occurred at 7:00 AM. At the dark hour of the morning, Tony would present an original meditation that would last about twenty minutes. It was definitely original, as you will observe; he regularly composed each one the night prior to presenting it. Meditation indeed! And of the highest calibre! The forty people who heard these unusual ideas and insights in the chapel were inspired to dialogue about them and apply them to their lives.

I have looked forward since my Maxi experience to seeing these meditations published. I think there must be at least a hundred more of these meditations in some nook or cranny, for Tony never missed morning meditation; for him meditation was fun; it was just another one of many delightful highlights in the day of a mystic.

Since receiving the first printing of Call To Love, I have used the meditations with more than fifty retreat groups with remarkable results. Depending on the variety of the congregation and the disposition of the individuals I have used abbreviated renditions and modified versions.

Each meditation in its entirety is most appropriate while one is engaged in the Ignatian Exercises, while on retreat, or when there is ample time for reflection.

I would recommend the highlighted version with people who are unfamiliar with de Mello's spirituality and with large groups. This shorter adaptation is also conducive for occasions when there are time restrictions.

May you enjoy many soul feelings and delight in the Divine Reality that surrounds you.

James R. Dolan,S.J.
Rochester, N.Y. 14618
U.S.A.

MEDITATION 1

WORLD FEELINGS VERSUS SOUL FEELINGS

For what will it profit a man, if he gains the whole world and forfeits his life? Mt. 16, 26

I. Recall the kind of feeling you have when someone praises you, when you are approved, accepted, applauded. And contrast that with the kind of feeling that arises within you when you look at the sunset or the sunrise, or Nature in general or when you read a book or watch a movie that you thoroughly enjoy. Get the taste of this feeling.

And *contrast* it with the first, namely, the one that was generated within you when you were praised. Understand that the first type of feeling comes from self-glorification, self-promotion. It is a worldly feeling. The second comes from self-fulfillment, a soul feeling.

II. Here is *another contrast:* Recall the kind of feeling you have when you succeed, when you have made it, when you get to the top, when you win a game or a bet or an argument.

And contrast it with the kind of feeling you get when you really enjoy the job you are doing, you are absorbed in, the action that you are currently engaged in. And once again notice the qualitative difference between the worldly feeling and the soul feeling.

III. *Yet another contrast:* Remember what you felt like when you had power, you were the boss, people looked up to you, took orders from you; or when you were popular. And contrast that worldly feeling with the feeling of intimacy, companionship — the times you thoroughly enjoyed yourself in the company of a friend or with a group in which there was fun and laughter.

A. Having done this, attempt to understand the true nature of worldly feelings, namely, the feelings of self-promotion, self-glorification. They are not natural.

> They were invented by your society and your culture to make you productive and to make you controllable. These feelings do not produce the nourishment and happiness that is produced when one contemplates Nature or enjoys the company of one's friends or one's work. They were meant to produce thrills, excitement and emptiness.

B. Then observe yourself in the course of a day or a week and think how many actions of yours are performed, how many activities engaged in that are uncontaminated by the desire for these thrills, these excitements that only produce emptiness, the desire for attention, approval, fame, popularity, success or power.

C. And take a look at the people around you. Is there a single one of them who has not become addicted to these worldly feelings?

> A single one who is not controlled by them, hungers for them, spends every minute of his/her waking life consciously or unconsciously seeking them?

When you see this you will understand how people attempt to gain the world and, in the process, lose their soul. For they live empty, soul-less lives.

And here is a parable of life for you to ponder on: A group of tourists sits in a bus that is passing through gorgeously beautiful country; lakes and mountains and greenfields and rivers. But the shades of the bus are pulled down. They do not have the slightest idea of what lies beyond the windows of the bus. And all the time of their journey is spent in squabbling over who will have the seat of honour in the bus, who will be applauded, who will be well considered. And so they remain till the journey's end.

MEDITATION 2

THE CAUSES OF UNHAPPINESS

If any one comes to me and does not hate his own father and mother and wife and children and brothers and sisters, yes, and even his own life, he cannot be my disciple.   Lk. 14.26

I.   Take a look at the world and see the unhappiness around you and in you. Do you know what causes this unhappiness?

> You will probably say loneliness or oppression or war or hatred or atheism. And you will be wrong.

There is only one cause of unhappiness: The false beliefs you have in your head, beliefs so widespread, so commonly held, that it never occurs to you to question them. Because of these false beliefs you see the world and yourself in a distorted way.

> Your programming is so strong and the pressure of society so intense that you are literally trapped into perceiving the world in this distorted kind of way.

There is no way out, because you do not even have a suspicion that your perception is distorted, your thinking is wrong, and your beliefs are false.

II.   Look around and see if you can find a single genuinely happy person — fearless, free from insecurities, anxieties, tensions, worries.

> You would be lucky if you found one in a hundred thousand. This should lead you to be suspicious of the programming and the beliefs that you and they hold in common. But you have also been programmed not to suspect, not to doubt, just to trust the assumptions that have been put into you by your tradition, your culture, your society, your religion. And if you are not happy, you have been trained to blame yourself, not your programming, not your cultural and inherited ideas and beliefs.

III.   What makes it even worse is the fact that most people are so brainwashed that they do not even realize how unhappy they are like the man in a dream who has no idea he is dreaming.

What are these false beliefs that block you from happiness? Here are some examples.

A.   *First belief:* You cannot be happy without the things that you are attached to and that you consider so precious.

False. There is not a single moment in your life when you do not have everything that you need to be happy.

Think of that for a minute.

The reason why you are unhappy is because you are focussing on what you do not have rather than on what you have right now.

B.   *Another belief:* Happiness is in the future.

Not true. Right here and now you are happy and you do not know it because your false beliefs and your distorted perceptions have got you caught up in fears, anxieties, attachments, conflicts, guilt and a host of games that you are programmed to play.

If you would see through this you would realize that you are happy and do not know it.

C.   *Yet another belief:* Happiness will come if you manage to change the situation you are in and the people around you.

Not true. You stupidly squander so much energy trying to rearrange the world.

If changing the world is your vocation in life, go right ahead and change it, but do not harbour the illusion that this is going to make you happy.

What makes you happy or unhappy is not the world and the people around you, but the thinking in your head.

As well search for an eagle's nest on the bed of an ocean, as search for happiness in the world outside of you.

So if it is happiness that you seek you can stop wasting your energy trying to cure your baldness or build up an attractive body or change your residence or job or community or lifestyle or even your personality.

Do you realize that you could change every one of these things, you could have the finest looks and the most charming personality and the most pleasant of surroundings and still be unhappy?

And deep down you know this is true but still you waste your effort and energy trying to get what you know cannot make you happy.

D.   *Another false belief :* If all your desires are fulfilled you will be happy.

Not true. In fact it is these very desires and attachments that make you tense, frustrated, nervous, insecure and fearful.

Make a list of all your attachments and desires and to each of them say these words: "Deep down in my heart I know that even after I have got you I will not get happiness."

And ponder on the truth of those words. The fulfillment of desire can, at the most, bring flashes of pleasure and excitement. Don't mistake that for happiness.

What then is happiness?

Very few people know and no one can tell you, because happiness cannot be described. Can you describe light to people who have been sitting in darkness all their lives? Can you describe reality to someone in a dream? Understand your darkness and it will vanish; then you will know what light is. Understand your nightmare for what it is and it will stop; then you will wake up to reality.

Understand your false beliefs and they will drop; then you will know the taste of happiness.

If people want happiness so badly, why don't they attempt to understand their false beliefs?

I.   First, because it never occurs to them to see them as false or even as beliefs.

They see them as facts and reality, so deeply have they been programmed.

II.   Second, because they are scared to lose the only world they know: the world of desires, attachments, fears, social pressures, tensions, ambitions, worries, guilt, with flashes of the pleasure and relief and excitement which these things bring.

Think of someone who is afraid to let go of a nightmare because, after all, that is the only world he knows. There you have a picture of yourself and of other people.

If you wish to attain to lasting happiness you must be ready to hate father, mother, even your own life and to take leave of all your possessions.

How? Not by renouncing them or giving them up because what you give up violently you are forever bound to. But rather by seeing them for the nightmare they are; and then, whether you keep them or not, they will have lost their grip over you, their power to hurt you, and you will be out of your dream at last, out of your darkness, your fear, your unhappiness.

Spend some time seeing each of the things you cling to for what it really is, a nightmare that causes you excitement and pleasure on the one hand but also worry, insecurity, tension, anxiety, fear, unhappiness on the other.

Father and mother: nightmare. Wife and children, brothers and sisters: nightmare. All your possessions: nightmare. Your life as it is now: nightmare. Every single thing you cling to and have convinced yourself you cannot be happy without: nightmare.

Then you will hate father and mother, wife and children, brothers and sisters and even your own life.

And you will so easily take leave of all your possessions, that is, you will stop clinging and thus have destroyed their capacity to hurt you.

Then at last you will experience that mysterious state that cannot be described or uttered the state of abiding happiness and peace. And you will understand how true it is that everyone who stops clinging to brothers or sisters, father, mother or children, land or houses.... is repaid a hundred times over and gains eternal life.

MEDITATION 3

DISCOVER THE PROGRAMME IN YOUR HEAD

And if any one would sue you and take your coat, let him have your cloak as well; and if any one forces you to go one mile, go with him two miles.   Mt. 5, 40-41

If you take a look at the way you have been put together and the way you function you will find that inside your head there is a whole programme, a set of demands about how the world should be, how you should be and what you should want.

Who is responsible for the programming? Not you.

> It isn't really you who decided even such basics as your wants and desires and so-called needs; your values, your tastes, your attitudes.

It was your parents, your society, your culture, your religion, your past experiences who fed the operating instructions into your computer.

> Now, however old you are or wherever you go, your computer goes along with you and is active and operating at each conscious

moment of the day, imperiously insisting that its demands be met by life, by people and by you.

If the demands are met, the computer allows you to be peaceful and happy. If they are not met, even though it be through no fault of yours, the computer generates negative emotions that cause you to suffer.

1. For instance, when other people don't live up to your computer's expectations, it torments you with frustration or anger or bitterness.

2. Another instance: when things are not under your control or the future is uncertain, your computer insists that you experience anxiety, tension, worry.

Then you expend a lot of energy coping with these negative emotions.

And you generally cope by expending more energy trying to rearrange the world around you so that the demands of your computer will be met.

If that happens you will be granted a measure of precarious peace; precarious because at any moment some trifle (a delayed train, a tape recorder that doesn't work, a letter that doesn't arrive — anything) is going to be out of conformity with your computer's programming and the computer will insist that you become upset again.

And so you live a pathetic existence, constantly at the mercy of things and people, trying desperately to make them conform to your computer's demands, so that you can enjoy the only peace you can ever know a temporary respite from negative emotions, courtesy of your computer and your programming.

Is there a way out? Yes.

You are not going to be able to change

your programming all that quickly, or perhaps ever. And you don't even need to.

Try this:

1.   Imagine you are in a situation or with a person that you find unpleasant and that you would ordinarily avoid.

2.   Now observe how your computer instinctively becomes active, insisting that you avoid this situation or try to change it.

3.   And if you stay on there and refuse to change the situation,

4.   Observe how the computer insists that you experience irritation or anxiety or guilt or some other negative emotion.

5.   Now keep looking at this unpleasant situation or person until you realize that:

A.   It isn't they that are causing the negative emotions.

B.   They are just going their way, being themselves, doing their thing whether right or wrong, good or bad.

C.   It is your computer that, thanks to your programming, insists on your reacting with negative emotions.

> You will see this better if you realize that someone with a different programming when faced with this same situation or person or event would react quite calmly, even happily. Don't stop till you have grasped this truth: the only reason why you too are not reacting calmly and happily is your computer that is stubbornly insisting that reality be reshaped to conform to its programming. Observe all of this from the outside so to speak and see the marvellous change that comes about in you.

Once you have understood this truth and thereby stopped your computer from generating negative emotions you may take any action you deem fit.

You may avoid the situation or the person; or you may try to change them; or you may insist on your rights or the rights of others being respected; you may even resort to the use of force.

But only after you have got rid of your emotional upsets, for then your action will spring from peace and love, not from the neurotic desire to appease your computer or to conform to its programming or to get rid of the negative emotions it generates.

Then you will understand how profound is the wisdom of the words: *"If a man wants to sue you for your shirt, let him have your coat as well. If a man in authority makes you go one mile, go with him two."*

For it will have become evident to you that real oppression comes, not from people who fight you in court or from authority that subjects you to slave labour, but from your computer whose programming destroys your peace of mind the moment outside circumstances fail to conform to its demands. People have been known to be happy even in the oppressive atmosphere of a concentration camp!

It is from the oppression of your programming that you need to be liberated.

Only then will you experience that inner freedom from which alone all social revolution must arise for the powerful emotion, the passion that arises in your heart at the sight of social evils and impels you to action, will have its origin in reality, not in your programming or your ego.

MEDITATION 4

UNDERSTAND YOUR PROGRAMME

And the young man went away sorrowful for he had great possessions. Mk. 10, 22

Has it ever struck you that you have been programmed to be unhappy and so no matter what you do to become happy, you are bound to fail?

It is as if you fed mathematical equations into a computer and then failed each time you pushed it to turn out lines from Shakespeare.

If you wish to be happy the first thing you need is not effort or even goodwill or good desires but a clear understanding of how exactly you have been programmed. This is what happened:

I.   First your society and your culture taught you to believe that you would not be happy without certain persons and certain things.

Just take a look around you: everywhere people have actually built their lives on the unquestioned belief that without certain things money, power, success, approval, a good reputation, love, friendship, spirituality, God they cannot be happy. What is your particular combination ?

II.   Once you swallowed your belief you naturally developed an attachment to this person or thing you were convinced you could not be happy without.

III.   Then came the efforts to acquire your precious thing or person, to cling to it once it was acquired, and to fight off every possibility of losing it.

IV.   This finally led you to abject emotional dependence so that the object of your attachment had the power to thrill you when you attained it, to make you anxious lest you be deprived of it and miserable when you lost it.

Stop for a moment now and contemplate in horror the endless list of attachments that you have become a prisoner to. Think of concrete things and persons, not abstractions...

Once your attachment had you in its grip you began to strive might and main, every waking minute of your life, to rearrange the world around you so that you could attain and maintain the objects of your attachment.

This is an exhausting task that leaves you little energy for the business of living and enjoying life fully. It is also an impossible task in an ever changing world that you simply are not able to control.

So instead of a life of serenity and fulfillment you are doomed to a life of frustration, anxiety, worry, insecurity, suspense, tension.

For a few fleeting moments the world does, indeed, yield to your efforts and rearranges itself to suit your desires.

Then you become briefly happy. Or rather, you experience a flash of pleasure which isn't happiness at all for it is accompanied by the underlying fear that at any moment this world of things and people that you have so painstakingly put in place will slip out of your control and let you down which it never fails to do sooner or later.

V.   And here is something else to ponder on: Each time you are anxious and afraid, it is because you may lose or fail to get the object of your attachment, isn't it?

> And each time you feel jealous, isn't it because someone may make off with what you are attached to? And almost all your anger comes from someone standing in the way of your attachment, doesn't it? And see how paranoid you become when your attachment is threatened — you cannot think objectively; your whole vision becomes distorted, doesn't it? And every time you feel bored, isn't it because you are not getting a sufficient supply of what you believe will make you happy, of what you are attached to?

And when you are depressed and miserable, the cause is there for all to see: life is not giving you what you have convinced yourself you cannot be happy without. Almost every negative emotion you experience is the direct outcome of an attachment.

So there you are loaded down by your attachments — and striving desperately to attain happiness precisely by holding on to the load. The very notion is absurd.

> The tragedy is that this is the only method that everyone has been taught for attaining happiness a method guaranteed to produce anxiety, disappointment and sorrow.

Hardly anyone has been told the following truth: in order to be genuinely happy there is one and only one thing you need to do: get deprogrammed, get rid of those attachments.

When people stumble upon this self-evident truth they become terrified at the thought of the pain involved in dropping their attachments. But the process is not a painful one at all. On the contrary...

Getting rid of attachments is a perfectly delightful task if the instrument you use to rid yourself of them is not will power or renunciation but sight.

All you need to do is:

1. Open your eyes and see that you do not really need the object of your attachment at all;

2. Just realize that you were programmed, brain-washed into thinking that you could not be happy or you could not live without this particular person or thing.

> Remember how heart-broken you once were, how you were certain you never would be happy again because you lost someone or something that was so precious to you? But then what happened? Time passed and you learnt to get on pretty well, did you not? That should have alerted you to the falseness of your belief, to the trick your programmed mind was playing on you.

An attachment isn't a fact. It is a belief, a fantasy in your head, acquired through programming.

> If that fantasy did not exist inside your head, you would not be attached. You would love things and persons and you would enjoy them thoroughly but, lacking the belief, you would enjoy them on a non-attachment basis.

> As a matter of fact, is there any other way to really enjoy something?

IV. Pass in review now all those attachments of yours. And to each person or object that comes to mind say: "I am not really attached to you at all. I am merely deluding myself into the belief that without you I will not be happy."

Just do this honestly and see the change that comes about within you:

> "I am not really attached to you at all. I have merely cheated myself into the belief that without you I will not be happy."

MEDITATION 5

YOUR MIND CAUSES UNHAPPINESS

*It is easier for a camel to go through the eye of a
needle than for a rich man to enter the kingdom
of God.*   Mk. 10, 25

What can one do to attain happiness? There is
nothing you or anyone else can do. Why? For the
simple reason that you are already happy right now.
So how can you acquire what you already have?

If that is so, why do you not experience this
happiness which is already yours? Because your
mind is creating unhappiness all the time. Drop this
unhappiness of your mind and the happiness that
has always been yours will instantly surface.

How does one drop unhappiness?

Find out what is causing it and look at the cause
unflinchingly. It will automatically drop.

Now if you look carefully, you will see that there is
one thing and only one thing that causes
unhappiness.

The name of that thing is Attachment.

What is an attachment?

An emotional state of clinging caused by the belief that without some particular thing or some person you cannot be happy.

This emotional state of clinging is composed of two elements, one positive and the other is negative. The positive element is the flash of pleasure and excitement, the thrill that you experience when you get what you are attached to. The negative element is the sense of threat and tension that always accompanies the attachment. Think of someone gobbling up food in a concentration camp; with one hand he brings the food to his mouth, with the other he protects it from neighbours who will grab it from him the moment he lowers his guard. There you have the perfect image of the attached person.

So an attachment by its very nature makes you vulnerable to emotional turmoil and is always threatening to shatter your peace.

So how can you expect an attached person to enter that ocean of happiness called the kingdom of God? As well expect a camel to pass through the eye of a needle!

Now the tragedy of an attachment is that if its object is not attained it causes unhappiness. But if it is attained, it does not cause happiness it merely causes a flash of pleasure followed by weariness; and it is always accompanied, of course, by the anxiety that you may lose the object of your attachment.

You will say, "Can't I keep just one attachment?" Of course. You can keep as many as you want. But for each attachment you pay a price in lost happiness.

Think of this: The nature of attachments is such, that even if you satisfy many of them in the course of a single day, the one attachment that was not satisfied will prey upon your mind and make you unhappy.

There is no way to win the battle of attachments. As well search for water without wetness as for an attachment without unhappiness.

No one has ever lived who has come up with a formula for keeping the objects of one's attachments without struggle, anxiety, fear and, sooner or later, defeat.

There is only one way to win the battle of attachments: Drop them.

Contrary to popular belief, dropping attachments is easy. All you have to do is see, but really see, the following truths.

I.   *First truth:* You are holding on to a false belief, namely, the belief that without this particular person or thing you will not be happy.

Take your attachments one at a time and see the falseness of this belief. You may encounter resistence from your heart, but the moment you do see, there will be an immediate emotional result. At that very instant the attachment loses its force.

II.   *Second truth:* If you just enjoy things, refusing to let yourself be attached to them, that is, refusing to hold the false belief that you will not be happy without them, you are spared all the struggle and emotional strain of protecting them and guarding them for yourself.

Has it occurred to you that you can keep all the objects of your attachments without giving them up, without renouncing a single one of them and you can enjoy them even more on a non-attachment, a non-clinging basis, because you are peaceful now and

relaxed and unthreatened in your enjoyment
of them?

III.   *The third and final truth:* If you learn to enjoy the
scent of a thousand flowers you will not cling to one
or suffer when you cannot get it.

If you have a thousand favourite dishes, the
loss of one will go unnoticed and leave your
happiness unimpaired. But it is precisely your
attachments that prevent you from developing
a wider and more varied taste for things and
people.

In the light of these three truths no attachment can
survive. But the light must shine uninterruptedly if
it is to be effective. Attachments can only thrive in
the darkness of illusion.

The rich man cannot enter the kingdom of joy
not because he wants to be bad but because
he chooses to be blind.

MEDITATION 6

CLINGING IS DYING

*Foxes have holes, and birds of the air have nests;
but the Son of man has nowhere to lay his head.*

Mt. 8, 20

Here is a mistake that most people make in their relationships with others. They try to build a steady nesting place in the ever moving stream of life.

Think of someone whose love you desire. Do you want to be important to this person, to be especial and make a difference to his/her life?

Do you want this person to care for you and be concerned about you in a special way? If you do, open your eyes and see that you are foolishly inviting others to reserve you for themselves, to restrict your freedom for their benefit, to control your behaviour, your growth and development so that it will suit their interest.

It is as if the other person said to you, "If you want to be especial to me then you must meet my conditions. Because the moment you cease to live up to my expectations, you will cease to be especial." You wanted to be especial to someone, didn't you? So you must pay a price in lost freedom. You must dance to the other person's tune just as you demand that other persons dance to yours if they want to be especial to you.

Pause now to ask yourself if it is worth paying so much for so little.

Imagine you say to this person whose special love you want, "Leave me free to be myself, to think my thoughts, to indulge my taste, to follow my inclination, to behave in ways that I decide are to my liking."

The moment you say those words you will understand that you are asking for the impossible. To ask to be especial to someone means essentially to be bound to the task of making yourself pleasing to this person. And therefore to lose your freedom. Take all the time you need to realize this.

May be now you are ready to say, "I'd rather have my freedom than your love." If you could either have company in prison or walk the earth in freedom all alone, which would you choose?

Now say to this person, "I leave you free to be yourself, to think your thoughts, to indulge your taste, follow your inclinations, behave in any way that you decide is to your liking."

The moment you say that you will observe one of two things:

1. Either your heart will resist those words and you will be exposed for the clinger and exploiter that you are (so now is the time to examine your false belief that without this person you cannot live or cannot be happy);

2. Or your heart will pronounce the words sincerely

and in that very instant all control, manipulation, exploitation, possessiveness, jealousy will drop. "I leave you free to be yourself: to think your thoughts, indulge your tastes, follow your inclinations, behave in ways that you decide are to your liking."

And you will notice something else:

3.   The person automatically ceases to be especial and important to you.

And he/she becomes important the way a sunset or a symphony is lovely in itself, the way a tree is especial in itself and not for the fruit or the shade that it can offer you. Your beloved will then belong not to you but to everyone or to no one like the sunrise and the tree.

> Test it by saying those words again: "I leave you free to be yourself... "

In saying those words you have set yourself free. You are now ready to love. For when you cling, what you offer the other is not love but a chain by which both you and your beloved are bound. Love can only exist in freedom. The true lover seeks the good of his beloved which requires especially the liberation of the beloved from the lover.

MEDITATION 7

THE VALUE OF NEGATIVE FEELINGS

The householder in anger said to his servant, 'Go out quickly to the streets and lanes of the city, and bring in the poor and maimed and blind and lame.'

Lk 14, 21

Think of someone you dislike — someone you generally avoid because his/her presence generates negative feelings in you. Imagine yourself in this person's presence now and watch the negative emotions arise...

You are, quite conceivably, in the presence of someone who is poor, crippled, blind or lame.

Now understand that if you invite this person, this beggar from the streets and alleys into your home, that is, into your presence, he/she will make you a gift that none of your charming, pleasant friends can make you, rich as they are.

He or she is going to reveal yourself to you and reveal human nature to you — a revelation as precious as any found in Scripture.

For what will it profit you to know all the

Scriptures if you do not know yourself and so live the life of a robot?

The revelation that this beggar is going to bring will widen your heart till there is room in it for every living creature.

Can there be a finer gift than that?

Now take a look at yourself reacting negatively and ask yourself the following question:

I. "Am I in charge of this situation or is this situation in charge of me?"

That is the first revelation. With it comes the second:

II. The way to be in charge of this situation is to be in charge of yourself, which you are not.

How does one achieve this mastery?

A. All you have to do is understand that there are people in the world who, if they were in your place, would not be negatively affected by this person.

B. They would be in charge of the situation, above it, not subject to it as you are.

III. Therefore, your negative feelings are caused, not by this person, as you mistakenly think, but by your programming. Here is the third and major revelation.

See what happens when you really understand this.

Having received these revelations about yourself, listen to this revelation concerning human nature.

This behaviour, this trait in the other person that causes you to react negatively — do you realize that he or she is not responsible for it?

You can hold on to your negative feelings only when

you mistakenly believe that he or she is free and aware and therefore responsible.

> But who ever did evil in awareness? The ability to do evil or to be evil is not freedom but a sickness for it implies a lack of consciousness and sensitivity. Those who are truly free cannot sin as God cannot sin.

This poor person here in front of you is crippled, blind, lame not stubborn and malicious as you so foolishly thought.

Understand this truth; look at it steadfastly and deeply; and you will see your negative emotions turn into gentleness and compassion.

> Suddenly you have room in your heart for someone who was consigned to the streets and alleys by others and by you.

> Now you will realize that this beggar came to your home with an alms for you — the widening of your heart in compassion and the release of your spirit in freedom.

Where before you used to be controlled (these persons had the power to create negative emotions in you and you go out of your way to avoid them) now you have the gift of freedom to avoid no one, to go anywhere.

> When you see this you will notice how to the feeling of compassion in your heart has been added the feeling of gratitude to this beggar who is your benefactor. And another new, unaccustomed feeling:

You actually feel a desire to seek out the company of these growth-producing crippled, blind and lame people, the way someone who has learnt to swim seeks water, because each time you are with them, where before you used to feel the oppression and tyranny of negative feelings, you can now actually feel an ever-expanding compassion and the freedom of the skies. And you can barely recognise yourself as you see yourself going out into the streets and alleys of the town, in obedience to the Master's injunction, to bring in the poor, the crippled, the blind and lame.

MEDITATION 8

ATTACHMENTS DRAIN US OF LIFE

*For judgment I came into this world, that those
who do not see may see, and that those who see
may become blind.*   *Jn. 9, 39*

It is said that love is blind. But is it? Actually
nothing on earth is as clearsighted as love. The
thing that is blind is not love but attachment. An
attachment is a state of clinging that comes from
the false belief that something or someone is
necessary for your happiness.

Do you have any attachment — people or
things that you falsely believe you could not
be happy without? Make a list of them right
now before we go on to study how exactly they
blind you.

Think of a politician who has convinced
himself he will not be happy unless he gets
political power. His quest for power coarsens
his sensitivity to the rest of life. He barely has
time for his family and friends. Suddenly all
human beings are perceived and reacted to in
terms of the support or threat that they are to
his ambition. And those who can neither

threaten nor support he does not even notice. If in addition to his craving for power he has an attachment to other things like sex or money, the poor man has become so selective in his perceptions that he could almost be said to be blind.

Everyone sees this except the man himself. This is the condition that leads to the rejection of the Messiah, the rejection of truth and beauty and goodness, because one has come to be blind to perceive them.

Now think of yourself listening to an orchestra in which the sound of the drum is so loud that nothing else can be heard. To enjoy the symphony you must be responsive to every instrument in the orchestra.

To be in the state called love you must be sensitive to the uniqueness and beauty of every single thing and person around you.

You can hardly be said to love what you not even notice; and if you notice only a few beings to the exclusion of others, that is not love at all.

For love excludes no one at all; it embraces the whole of life; it listens to the symphony as a whole, not to just one or the other of the musical instruments.

Stop for a while now to see how your attachments drain life's symphony no less than the politician's attachment to power and the businessman's attachment to money have hardened them to the melody of life.

Or look at the matter in another way:

There is an enormous amount of information that is continuously flowing in from the world through the senses, the tissues of the organs of your body.

Only a small part of this information reaches your conscious mind. It is like the infinite amount of feedback that is sent to the President of a nation: only a tiny fraction finally makes its way to him. Somebody does the screening and the processing at the President's office.

Who decides what will finally make its way to your conscious mind from all the material that is pouring in from the world? Three decisive filters: First your attachments, second your beliefs and third your fears.

I.   *Your attachments:* You will inevitably look for what fosters or threatens them and turn a blind eye to the rest.

> You won't be interested in the rest any more than the avaricious businessman is interested in anything that does not involve the making of money.

II.   *Your beliefs:* Just take a look at a fanatic who only notices what confirms his/her belief and blocks out whatever threatens it and you will understand what your beliefs are doing to you.

III. And then *your fears:*

> If you knew you were to be executed in a week's time it would wonderfully concentrate your mind to the exclusion of everything else. That is what fears do.

They irresistibly rivet your attention on to some things to the exclusion of others.

IV.   You falsely think:

A.   that your fears protect you,

B.   that your beliefs have made you what you are and

C.   that your attachments make your life exciting and secure.

You fail to see that they are actually a screen between you and life's symphony.

It is quite impossible, of course, to be fully conscious of every note in life's symphony.

But if your spirit becomes unclogged and your senses open, you will begin to perceive things as they really are and to interact with reality and you will be entranced by the harmonies of the universe. Then you will understand what God is, for you will at last know what love is.

Look at it this way: You see persons and things not as they are but as you are.

If you wish to see them as they are you must attend to your attachments and the fears that your attachments generate. Because when you look at life it is these attachments and fears that will decide what you will notice and what you block out. Whatever you notice then commands your attention. And since your looking has been selective you have an illusory version of the things and people around you.

The more you live with this distorted version the more you become convinced that it is the only true picture of the world because your attachments and fears continue to process incoming data in a way that will reinforce your picture.

This is what gives origin to your beliefs: fixed, unchanging ways of looking at a reality which is not fixed and unchanging at all but in movement and change. So it is no longer the real world that you interact with and love but a world created by your head. It is only when you drop your beliefs, your fears and the attachments that breed them that you will be freed from the insensitivity that makes you so deaf and blind to yourself and to the world.

MEDITATION 9

DROPPING ATTACHMENTS

Repent, for the kingdom of heaven is at hand.

Mt. 4, 17

Imagine you have a radio that no matter how you turn the knob picks up only one station. You have no control over the volume. At times the sound is barely audible, at others, it is so loud that it almost shatters your eardrums. Moreover it is impossible to turn it off; at times it will be slow; it will suddenly begin to blare away when you want to rest and sleep.

Who would put up with this kind of performance in a radio? And yet when your heart behaves in this kind of crazy fashion you not only put up with it but even call it normal and human.

Think of the numerous times you were tossed about by your emotions, that you have suffered the pangs of anger, depression, anxiety, when in every instance it was because your heart became set on getting something that you did not have, or on holding on to something that you had, or on avoiding something that you did not want.

You were in love and you felt rejected or jealous; suddenly all your mind and heart became focussed on this one thing, and the banquet of life turned to ashes in your mouth. You were bent on winning an election and in the din of battle it was impossible to hear the songs of birds: your ambition drowned out every other sound. You were faced with the possibility of a serious illness, or the loss of a loved one and you found it impossible to concentrate on anything.

To put it briefly, the moment you pick up an attachment, the functioning of this lovely apparatus called the human heart is destroyed.

If you want to repair your radio, you must study radio mechanics.

If you want to reform your heart, you must give serious, prolonged thought to four liberating truths. But first choose some attachment that troubles you, something that you are clinging to, or something that you dread, or something you are craving for, and keep this attachment in mind as you listen to these truths.

I.   *The first truth:* You must choose between your attachment and happiness. You cannot have both. The moment you pick up an attachment, your heart is thrown out of kilter and your ability to lead a joyful carefree serene life is destroyed.

·See how true this is when applied to the attachment that you have chosen.

II.   *The second truth:* Where did your attachment come from? You were not born with it. It sprang from a lie that your society and your culture have told you, or a lie that you have told yourself, namely, that without this or the other, without this person or the other, you can't be happy.

Just open your eyes and see how false this is. There are hundreds of persons who are perfectly happy without this thing or person or situation that you crave for and that you have convinced yourself you cannot live without. So make your choice: Do you want your attachment, or your freedom and happiness.

III.   *The third truth:* If you wish to be fully alive you must develop a sense of perspective. Life is infinitely greater than this trifle your heart is attached to and which you have given the power to so upset you.

Trifle? Yes, because if you live long enough, a day will easily come when it will cease to matter. It will not even be remembered — your own experience will confirm this. Just as today you barely remember, are no longer the least bit affected by those tremendous trifles that so disturbed you in the past.

IV.   And so the *fourth truth* brings you to the unavoidable conclusion, that no thing or person outside of you has the power to make you happy or unhappy. Whether you are aware of it or not it is you and only you, who decides to be happy or unhappy, whether you will cling to your attachment or not in any given situation.

As you ponder these truths, you may become aware that your heart is resisting them or argues against them and refuses to look at them. That is a sign that you have not yet suffered enough at the hand of your attachments to really want to do something about your spiritual radio. Or your heart may place no resistance to these truths; if that is so, rejoice. Repentance, the refashioning of the heart has begun and the kingdom of God — the gratefully carefree life of children — has come within your grasp at last and you are about to reach out and take possession of it.

MEDITATION 10

LIFE IS A SYMPHONY

*Teacher, what good deed must I do, to have
eternal life?*   *Mt. 19, 16*

Think of yourself in a concert hall listening to
the strains of the sweetest music when you
suddenly remember that you forgot to lock
your car. You are anxious about the car, you
cannot walk out of the hall and you cannot
enjoy the music. There you have a perfect
image of life as it is lived by most human
beings.

Life to those who have the ears to hear is a
symphony; but very, very rare indeed is the human
being who hears the music. Why? Because they are
busy listening to the noises that their conditioning
and their programming have put into their heads.
That and something else — their attachments. An
attachment is a major killer of life.

To really hear the symphony you must be
sensitively attuned to every instrument in the
orchestra. When you take pleasure only in the
drum, you cease to hear the symphony
because the sound of the drum has blotted

out the other instruments. You may have your preferences for drum or violin, or piano; no harm in these, for a preference does not damage your capacity to hear and enjoy the other instruments. But the moment your preference turns into an attachment, it hardens you to the other sounds, you suddenly undervalue them. And it blinds you to its particular instrument, for you give it a value out of all proportion to its merit.

Now look at a person or a thing you have an attachment for: someone or something to whom you have handed over the power to make you happy or unhappy. Observe how, because of your concentration on getting this person or thing and holding onto it and enjoying it exclusively to the exclusion of other things and persons, you have less sensitivity to the rest of the world.

Observe how, because of your obsession with this person or thing, You have become hardened.

Have the courage to see how prejudiced and blind you have become in the presence of this object of your attachment.

When you see this you will feel a yearning to rid yourself of every attachment. The problem is, how?

Renunciation and avoidance is no help, for to blot out the sound of the drum once again makes you as hard and insensitive as to concentrate solely on the drum.

What you need is not renunciation but understanding, awareness.

A. If your attachments have caused you suffering and sorrow, that's a help to understanding.

B. If you have at least once in your life had the sweet taste of freedom and the delight in life that unattachment brings, that too is a help.

C.   It also helps to consciously notice the sound of the other instruments in the orchestra.

D.   But there is no substitute for the awareness that shows you the loss you suffer when you overvalue the drum and when you turn a deaf ear to the rest of the orchestra.

The day that happens and your attachment to the drum drops, you will no longer say to your friend, "How happy you have made me." For in so saying you flatter his ego and manipulate him into wanting to please you again. And you give yourself the illusion that your happiness depends on your friend.

Rather you will say, "When you and I met, happiness arose."

> That leaves the happiness not contaminated by his ego and yours. Neither of you can take the credit for it. And that makes it possible for the two of you to part with no attachment to each other, or to the experience which your meeting generated, for you have enjoyed, not each other, but the symphony that arose in your meeting.

And when you move on to the next situation, or person, or work, you do so without any emotional carry over. And then you make the joyful discovery that the symphony arises there too, playing a different melody in the next situation, and the next, and the next.

Now you will move through life living from one moment to the other, wholly absorbed in the present, carrying with you so little from the past that your spirit could pass through the eye of a needle; as little distracted by the worries of the future as the birds of the air and the flowers of the field. You will be attached to no person or thing, for you will have developed a taste for the symphony of life. And you will love life alone with the passionate attachment of your whole heart and your whole soul and your whole mind and all your strength. You will find yourself travelling unencumbered and free as a bird in the sky, always living in the Eternal Now. And you will have found in your heart the answer to the question, "Master, what is it that I must do to get eternal life?"

MEDITATION 11

LAYERS ON THE BRAIN

When his disciples came to point out to him the buildings of the temple, he answered them 'You see all these, do you not? Truly, I say to you, there will not be left here one stone upon another, that will not be thrown down.' Mt. 24, 1-2

Think of a flabby person covered with layers of fat. That is what your mind can become — flabby, covered with layers of fat till it becomes too dull and lazy to think, to observe, to explore, to discover. It loses its alertness, its aliveness, its flexibility and goes to sleep.

Look around you and you will see almost everyone with minds like that: dull, asleep, protected by layers of fat, not wanting to be disturbed or questioned into wakefulness.

What are these layers?

Every belief that you hold, every conclusion you have reached about persons and things, every habit and every attachment.

In your formative years you should have been

helped to scrape off these layers and liberate your mind. Instead your society, your culture, which put these layers on your mind in the first place, has educated you to not even notice them, to go to sleep and let other people — the experts: your politicians, your cultural and religious leaders do your thinking for you.

So you are weighed down with the load of unexamined, unquestioned authority and tradition.

Let us examine these layers one at a time.

I.   *First: your beliefs.*

You experience life as a communist or a capitalist, as a Moslem or a Jew, you are experiencing life in a prejudiced, slanted way; there is a barrier, a layer of fat between Reality and you because you no longer see and touch it directly.

> If you experience life as a communist or a capitalist, as a Moslem or a Jew, you are experiencing life in a prejudiced, slanted way.

II. *Second layer: Your ideas.*

If you hold on to an idea about someone, then you no longer love that person but your idea of that person.

> You see him/her do or say something or behave in a certain kind of way, and you slap a label on: "She is silly or he is dull or he is cruel or she is very sweet," etc.

So now you have a screen, a layer of fat between you and this person because when you next meet him/her you will experience them in terms of that idea of yours even though they have changed.

> Observe how you have done this with almost everyone you know.

III.   *Third layer: Your habits.*

A habit is essential to human living. How would we
ever walk or speak or drive a car unless we relied on
habit? But habits must be limited to things
mechanical — not to love or to sight. Who wants to
be loved from habit?

> Have you ever sat on a seashore spellbound
> by the majesty and the mystery of the ocean?
> A fisherman looks at the ocean daily and does
> not notice its grandeur. Why? The dulling
> effect of a layer of fat called habit.

You have formed fixed ideas of all the things you see
and, when encountering them, it is not them you
see in all their changing freshness, but the same
dull, thick, boring idea acquired through habit. And
that is how you deal with people and with things,
how you relate to them: no freshness, no newness,
but the same dull, routine (boring) ways produced
by habit.

> You are incapable of looking in other, more
> creative ways, for, having developed a habit
> for dealing with the world and with people,
> you can put your mind on automatic pilot and
> go to sleep.

IV.   *Fourth layer: Your attachments and your fears.*

This layer is the easiest to see. Put a thick coating of
attachment, of fear (and therefore dislike) on to
anything or anyone — in that very instant you cease
to see that person or thing as it really is.

> Just recall some of the persons you dislike or
> fear or are attached to and you will see how
> true this is.

Do you see now how you are in a prison created by
the beliefs and traditions of your society and culture
and by the ideas, prejudices, attachments and fears
of your past experiences?

Wall upon wall surrounds your prison cell so that it seems almost impossible that you will ever break out and make contact with the richness of life and love and freedom that lies beyond your prison fortress. And yet the task, far from being impossible, is actually easy and delightful.

What can you do to break out? Four things:

I. *First*, realize that you are surrounded by prison walls, that your mind has gone to sleep. It does not even occur to most people to see this, so they live and die as prison inmates.

Most people end up being conformists; they adapt to prison life. A few become reformers; they fight for better living conditions in the prison, better lighting, better ventilation. Hardly anyone becomes a rebel, a revolutionary who breaks down the prison walls.

You can only be a revolutionary when you see the prison walls in the first place.

II. *Second*, contemplate the walls, spend hours just observing your ideas, your habits, your attachments and your fears without any judgment and condemnation. Look at them and they will crumble.

III. *Third*, spend some time observing the things and people around you. Look, but really look, as if for the very first time, at the face of a friend, a leaf, a tree, a bird in flight, the behaviour and mannerism of the people around you.

Really see them and hopefully you will see them afresh as they are in themselves without the dulling, stupefying effect of your ideas and habits.

D. The *fourth and most important step:* Sit down quietly and observe how your mind functions. There is a steady flow of thoughts and feelings and reactions there. Watch the whole of it for long stretches of time the way you watch a river or a movie. You will soon find it so much more absorbing than any river or movie. And so much more life-giving and liberating.

> After all can you even be said to be alive if you are not even conscious of your own thoughts and reactions?

> The unaware life, it is said, is not worth living. It cannot even be called life; it is a mechanical, robot existence; a sleep, an unconsciousness, a death; and yet this is what people call human life!

So watch, observe, question, explore and your mind will come alive and shed its fat and become keen and alert and active. Your prison walls will come tumbling down till not one stone of the Temple will be left upon another, and you will be blessed with the unimpeded vision of things as they are, the direct experience of Reality.

MEDITATION 12

THE QUALITIES OF HOLINESS

*When you give alms, do not let your left hand
know what your right hand is doing.*   Mt. 6, 3

It is with charity as with happiness and holiness. It
is not possible for you to say that you are happy
because the moment you become conscious of your
happiness you cease to be happy.

What you call the experience of happiness is not
happiness at all but the excitement and thrill
caused by some person or thing or event.

True happiness is uncaused. You are happy for no
reason at all.

And true happiness cannot be experienced. It is not
within the realm of consciousness. So it is with
holiness.

I.   Holiness is unself-consciousness.

The moment you are aware of your holiness it goes
sour and becomes self-righteousness.

A good deed is never so good as when you
have no consciousness that it is good — you
are so much in love with the action that you

are quite unselfconscious about your goodness and virtue. Your left hand has no idea that your right hand is doing something good or meritorious. You simply do it because it seems the natural, spontaneous thing to do.

Spend some time in becoming aware of the fact that all the virtue that you can see in yourself is no virtue at all but something that you have cunningly cultivated and produced and forced on yourself. If it were real virtue you would have enjoyed it thoroughly and would feel so natural that it wouldn't occur to you to think of it as a virtue. So the first quality of holiness is its unself-consciousness.

II. *The second quality is its effortlessness.*

Effort can change behaviour, it cannot change you.

Think of this: Effort can put food into your mouth, it cannot produce an appetite; it can keep you in bed, it cannot produce sleep; it can make you reveal a secret to another but it cannot produce trust; it can force you to pay a compliment, it cannot produce genuine admiration;

Effort can perform acts of service, it is powerless to produce love or holiness. All you can achieve by your effort is repression, not genuine change and growth. Change is only brought about by awareness and understanding. Understand your unhappiness and it will disappear — what results is the state of happiness.

Understand your pride and it will drop — what results will be humility. Understand your unhappiness, and it will disappear — what results is the state of happiness. Understand your fears and they will melt — the resultant state is love. Understand your attachments and they will vanish—the consequence is freedom.

Love and freedom and happiness are not things that you can cultivate and produce. You cannot even know what they are. All you can do is observe their opposites and, through your observation, cause these opposites to die.

III.   There is a *third quality of holiness:* It cannot be desired. If you desire happiness you will be anxious lest you do not attain it.

> You will be constantly in a state of dissatisfaction; and dissatisfaction and anxiety kill the very happiness that they set out to gain.

When you desire holiness for yourself you feed the very greed and ambition that make you so selfish and vain and unholy.

Here is something you must understand: There are two sources for change within you.

1.   One is the cunningness of your ego that pushes you into making efforts to become something other than you are meant to be so that it can give itself a boost, so that it can glorify itself.

2.   The other is the wisdom of Nature. Thanks to this wisdom you become aware, you understand it. That is all you do, leaving the change — type, the manner, the speed, the time of change to Reality and to Nature.

> Your ego is a great technician. It cannot be creative. It goes in for methods and techniques and produces so-called holy people who are rigid, consistent, mechanical, lifeless, as intolerant of others as they are of themselves, violent people — the very opposite of holiness and love. The type of "spiritual" people who, conscious of their spirituality, then proceed to crucify the Messiah.

Nature is not a technician. Nature is creative. You

will be a creator, not a wily technician when there is abandonment in you — no greed, no ambition, no anxiety, no sense of striving, gaining, arriving, attaining. All there is, is a keen, alert, penetrating, vigilant awareness that causes the dissolution of all one's foolishness and selfishness, all one's attachments and fears.

The changes that follow are not the result of your blueprints and efforts but the product of Nature that spurns your plans and will, thereby leaving no room for a sense of merit or achievement, or even any consciousness on the part of your left hand of what Reality is doing by means of your right.

MEDITATION 13

THE WAY OF NATURE

So be wise as serpents and innocent as doves.

Mt. 10, 16

Observe the wisdom that operates in doves and in flowers and trees and the whole of nature.

It is the same wisdom that does for us what our brain could never do: it circulates our blood, digests our food, pumps our hearts, expands our lungs, immunises our bodies and heals our wounds while our conscious minds are engaged in other matters.

This kind of nature-wisdom we are only now beginning to discover in so-called primitive peoples who, like the dove, are so simple and wise.

We who consider ourselves more advanced have developed another kind of wisdom, the cunningness of the brain, for we have realized that we can improve on Nature and provide ourselves with safety and protection and length of life and speed and comfort unknown to primitive peoples. All of this thanks to a fully developed brain. Our challenge is to recapture the simplicity and wisdom of the dove without losing the cunningness of the serpentine brain.

How can you achieve this? Through an important realization, namely, that every time you strive to improve on Nature by going against it, you will damage yourself for Nature is your very being.

It is as if your right hand were to fight your left hand or your right foot were to stamp on your left foot. Both sides lose and, instead of being creative and alive, you are locked in conflict. This is the state of most people in the world. Take a look at them: dead, uncreative, stuck because they are locked in conflict with nature, attempting to improve themselves by going against what their nature demands.

In a conflict between Nature and your brain, back Nature; if you fight her, she will eventually destroy you.

The secret therefore is to improve on Nature in harmony with Nature. How can you achieve this harmony?

I.   *First:* Think of some change that you wish to bring about in your life or in your personality. Are you attempting to force this change on your nature through effort and through the desire to become something that your ego has planned? That is the serpent fighting the dove.

Or are you content to study, observe, understand, be aware of your present state and problems, without pushing, without forcing things that your ego desires, leaving Reality to effect changes according to Nature's plans, not yours? Then you have the perfect blending of the serpent and the dove.

Take a look at some of those problems of yours, those changes you desire in yourself, and observe your way of going about it. See how you attempt to bring about change both in yourself and in others through the use of punishment and reward, through discipline and control, through sermonizing and guilt, through greed and pride, ambition and vanity, rather than through loving acceptance and patience, painstaking understanding and vigilant awareness.

II.   *Second:* Think of your body and compare it with the body of an animal that is left in its natural habitat. The animal is never overweight, never tense except before fight or flight.

> It never eats or drinks what is not good for it. It has all the rest and exercise that it needs. It has the right amount of exposure to the elements, to wind and sun and rain and heat and cold.

That is because the animal listens to its body and allows itself to be guided by the body's wisdom. Compare that with your own foolish cunningness. If your body could speak, what would it say to you?

> Observe the greed, the ambition, the vanity, the desire to show off and to please others, the guilt that drives you to ignore the voice of your body while you chase after objectives set by your ego. You have indeed lost the simplicity of the dove.

III.   *Third:* Ask yourself how much you are in touch with Nature, with trees and earth and grass and sky and wind and rain and sun and flowers and birds and animals. How much are you exposed to Nature? How much do you commune with her, observe her, contemplate her in wonder, identify with her?

> When your body is too long withdrawn from the elements, it withers, it becomes flabby and fragile because it has been isolated from its life force.

When you are too long separated from Nature, your spirit withers and dies because it has been wrenched from its roots.

MEDITATION 14

GRACEFUL CHANGE

*The kingdom of heaven has suffered violence, and
men of violence take it by force.*   *Mt. 11, 12*

Compare the serene and simple splendour of a rose
in bloom with the tensions and restlessness of your
life. The rose has a gift that you lack: it is perfectly
content to be itself. It has not been programmed
from birth, as you have been, to be dissatisfied with
itself, so it has not the slightest urge to be anything
other than it is.

That is why it possesses the artless grace and
absence of inner conflict that among humans
is only found in little children and mystics.

Consider your sad condition. You are always
dissatisfied with yourself, always wanting to change
yourself. So you are full of violence and
self-intolerance which only grows with every effort
that you make to change yourself. So any change you
achieve is always accompanied by inner conflict.

And you suffer when you see others achieve
what you have not and become what you are
not.

Would you be tormented by jealousy and envy
if, like the rose, you were content to be what
you are and never aspired to what you are
not? But you are driven, are you not, to be
like someone else who has more knowledge,
better looks, more popularity or success than
you. You want to become more virtuous, more
loving, more meditative; you want to find God,
to come closer to your ideals.

Think of the sad history of your efforts at
self-improvement, that either ended in disaster or
succeeded only at the cost of struggle and pain.

Now suppose you desisted from all efforts to
change   yourself,   and   from   all
self-dissatisfaction,   would   you   then   be
doomed to go to sleep having passively
accepted everything in you and around you?

There is another way besides laborious self-pushing
on the one hand and stagnant acceptance on the
other. It is the way of self-understanding. This is far
from easy because to understand what you are
requires complete freedom from all desire to change
what you are into something else.

You will see this if you compare the attitude of
a scientist who studies the habits of ants
without the slightest desire to change them
with the attitude of a dog trainer who studies
the habits of a dog with a view to making it
learn something.

If what you attempt is not to change yourself but to
observe yourself, to study everyone of your reactions
to people and things, without judgement or
condemnation or desire to reform yourself, your
observation will be non-selective, comprehensive,
never fixed in rigid conclusions, always open and
fresh from moment to moment.

Then you will notice a marvellous thing happening

within you: you will be flooded with the light of awareness, you will become transparent and transformed.

Will change occur then? Oh, yes. In you and in your surroundings.

But it will not be brought about by your cunning, restless ego that is forever competing, comparing, coercing, sermonizing, manipulating in its intolerance and its ambitions, thereby creating tension and conflict and resistance between you and Nature an exhausting, self-defeating process like driving with your brakes on.

The transforming light of awareness brushes aside your scheming, self-seeking ego to give Nature full rein to bring about the kind of change that she produces in the rose: artless, graceful, unself-conscious, wholesome, untainted by inner conflict. Since all change is violent she will be violent. But the marvellous quality of Nature-violence, unlike ego-violence, is that it does not spring from intolerance and self-hatred.

So there is no anger in the rainstorm that carries everything before it, or the fish that devour their young in obedience to ecological laws we know not, or body cells when they destroy each other in the interest of a higher good.

When Nature destroys, it is not from ambition or greed or self-aggrandisement, but in obedience to mysterious laws that seek the good of the whole universe above the survival and well-being of the parts.

It is this kind of violence that arises within mystics who storm against ideas and structures that have become entrenched in their societies and cultures when awareness awakens them to evils their contemporaries are blind to.

It is this violence that causes the rose to come into being in the face of forces hostile to it. And it is to this violence that the rose, like the mystic, will sweetly succumb after it has opened its petals to the sun and lives in fragile, feeling loveliness, quite unconcerned to add a single extra minute to its allotted span of life. And so it lives in blessedness and beauty like the birds of the air and the flowers of the field, with no trace of the restlessness and dissatisfaction, the jealousy and anxiety and competitiveness that characterize the world of human beings who seek to control and coerce rather than be content to flower into awareness, leaving all charge to the mighty force of God in Nature.

MEDITATION 15

LOVE IS FOUND IN FREEDOM

*Teacher, they said, we know that you speak and
teach rightly, and show no partiality.* Lk. 20, 21

Look at your life and see how you have filled its
emptiness with people. As a result they have a
stranglehold on you. See how they control your
behaviour by their approval and disapproval.

They hold the power to ease your loneliness with
their company, to send your spirits soaring with
their praise, to bring you down to the depths with
their criticism and rejection.

Take a look at yourself spending almost every
waking minute of your day placating and pleasing
people, whether they are living or dead.

> You live by their norms, conform to their
> standards, seek their company, desire their
> love, dread their ridicule, long for their
> applause, meekly submit to the guilt they lay
> upon you; you are terrified to go against the
> fashion in the way you dress or speak or act
> or even think.

> And observe how even when you control them

you depend on them and are enslaved by them.

People have become so much a part of your being that you cannot even imagine living a life that is unaffected or uncontrolled by them. As a matter of fact, they have convinced you that if you ever broke free of them, you would become an island — solitary, bleak, unloving. But the exact opposite is true.

How can you love someone whom you are a slave to? How can you love someone whom you cannot live without? You can only desire, need, depend and fear and be controlled. Love is to be found only in fearlessness and freedom. How do you achieve this freedom? By means of a two-pronged attack on your dependency and slavery.

I. *First, awareness.* It is next to impossible to be dependent, to be a slave, when one constantly observes the folly of one's dependence. But awareness may not be enough for a person whose addiction is people.

II. You must cultivate activities that you love. You must discover work that you do, not for its utility, but for itself.

> Think of something that you love to do for itself, whether it succeeds or not, whether you are praised for it or not, whether you are loved and rewarded for it or not, whether people know about it and are grateful to you for it or not.

How many activities can you count in your life that you engage in simply because they delight you and grip your soul? Find them out, cultivate them, for they are your passport to freedom and to love.

Here too you have probably been brainwashed into the following consumeristic way of thinking:

> To enjoy a poem or a landscape or a piece of

music seems a waste of time; you must produce a poem or a composition or a work of art. Even to produce it is of little value in itself; your work must be known. What good is it if no one ever knows it? And even if it is known, that means nothing if it is not applauded and praised by people. Your work achieves maximum value if it becomes popular and sells! So you are back again into the arms and control of people.

The value of an action, according to them, is not in its being loved and done and enjoyed for itself, but in its success.

The royal road to mysticism and to Reality does not pass through the world of people. It passes through the world of actions that are engaged in for themselves without an eye to success or to gain or profit actions.

Contrary to popular beliefs, the cure for lovelessness and loneliness is not company but contact with Reality. The moment you touch this Reality you will know what freedom and love are. Freedom from people and so the ability to love them.

You must not think for love to arise in your heart, you must first meet people. That would not be love but attraction or compassion. Rather it is love that first springs in the heart through your contact with the Real. Not love for any particular person or thing but the reality of love an attitude, a disposition of love. This love then radiates outwards to the world of things and persons.

If you desire this love to exist in your life you must break loose from your inward dependence on people by becoming aware of it and by engaging in activities that you love to do for themselves.

MEDITATION 16

YOUR ONE TRUE TEACHER

But you are not to be called rabbi, for you have one teacher, and you are all brethren. Mt. 20, 8

You can get someone to teach you things mechanical or scientific or mathematical like Algebra or English or riding a cycle or operating a computer.

But in the things that really matter, life, love, reality, God, no one can teach you a thing. All they can do is give you formulas. And as soon as you have a formula, you have reality filtered through the mind of someone else. If you take those formulas you will be imprisoned. You will wither and when you come to die you will not have known what it means to see for yourself, to learn.

Look at it this way: There have been moments in your life when you had an experience that you know you will have to carry with you to your grave because you are quite unable to find words with which to communicate the experience to anyone. As a matter of fact there simply are no words in any human language to communicate exactly what you experienced.

Think of the kind of feeling that came upon you when you saw a bird fly over a lake or observed a blade of grass peeping out of a crack in the wall or heard the cry of a baby at night or sensed the loveliness of a naked human body or gazed at a corpse lying cold and rigid in a coffin. You may try to communicate the experience in music or poetry or painting. But in your heart you know that no one will ever comprehend exactly what it was you saw and sensed. This is something you are quite powerless to express, much less teach, to another human being.

That is exactly how a Master feels when you ask him to teach you about life or God or reality. All he can do is give you a formula, a set of words strung together into a formula. But of what use are those words?

> Imagine a group of tourists in a bus. The shades of the bus are down and they don't see or hear or touch or smell a single of the strange exotic country that they are passing through, while all the while their guide chatters away, giving them what he thinks is a vivid description of the smells, sounds and sights of the world outside. The only thing they will experience are the images that his words create in their heads. And let's suppose the bus stops and he sends them forth with formulas about what they can expect to see and experience. Their experience will be contaminated, conditioned, distorted by those formulas and they will perceive, not the Reality itself but Reality as filtered through the guide's formulas.
>
> They will look at Reality selectively or they will project their own formulas on to it, so it is not Reality they will see but a confirmation of their formulas.

Is there any way you can know that what you are in touch with is Reality. Here is one sign: What you perceive does not fit into any formula whether given by another or created by yourself: it simply cannot be put into words.

So what can teachers do? They can bring to your notice what is unreal, they cannot show you Reality; they can destroy your formulas, they cannot make you see what the formula is pointing to; they can indicate your error, they cannot put you in possession of the Truth.

They can, at the most, point in the direction of Reality, they cannot tell you what to see.

You will have to walk out there all alone and discover for yourself.

To walk alone that means to walk away from every formula the ones given to you by others, the ones you learnt from books, the ones that you yourself invented in the light of your own past experience. That is possibly the most terrifying thing a human being can do: move into the unknown, unprotected by any formula.

To walk away from the world of human beings as the prophets and the mystics did is not to walk away from their company but from their formulas. Then, even though you are surrounded by people, you are truly and utterly alone.

What an awesome solitude! That solitude, that aloneness is Silence. It is only this Silence that you will see. And the moment you see you will abandon every book and guide and guru.

What is it that you will see? Anything, everything: a falling leaf, the behaviour of a friend, the ripples on the surface of a lake, a pile of stones, a ruined building, a crowded street, a starry sky, whatever. After you have seen, someone may attempt to help you put your vision into words but you will shake your head No, not that that's just another formula. Someone else will attempt to explain the meaning of what you saw and you will shake your head again because meaning is a formula, something that can be put into concepts and makes sense to the thinking mind, and what you saw is beyond all formula, all meaning. And a strange change will come about in you, barely perceptible at first but radically transforming. Because, having seen, you will never be the same again. You will feel the exhilarating freedom, the extraordinary confidence that comes from knowing that every formula, no matter how sacred, is worthless; and you will never again call anyone your teacher. Then you will never cease to learn as each day you observe and understand afresh the whole process and movement of life. Then every single thing will be your teacher.

So put your books and formulas aside; dare to abandon your teacher whoever your teacher may be and see things for yourself.

Dare to look at everything around you without fear and without formula and it won't be long before you see.

MEDITATION 17

INNOCENCE REGAINED

*Truly, I say to you, unless you turn and become
like children, you will never enter the kingdom of
heaven.*   Mt. 18, 3

The first quality that strikes one when one looks
into the eyes of a child is its innocence: its lovely
inability to lie or wear a mask or pretend to be
anything other than what it is. In this the child is
exactly like the rest of nature.

A dog is a dog; a rose, a rose; a star, a star;
everything is quite simply what it is.

Only the adult human being is able to be one thing
and pretend to be another.

I.   When grown-ups punish a child for telling the truth,
for revealing what it thinks and feels, the child
learns to dissemble and its innocence is destroyed.

Soon it will join the ranks of the numberless
people who say helplessly, " I do not know
who I am," for, having hidden the truth about
themselves for so long from others, they end
up by hiding it from themselves.

How much of the innocence of childhood do you still retain? Is there anyone today in whose presence you can be simply and totally yourself, as nakedly open and innocent as a child?

II.   There is another more subtle way in which the innocence of childhood is lost: when the child is infected by the desire to become somebody.

Contemplate the crowds of people who are striving might and main to become, not what Nature intended them to be — musicians, cooks, mechanics, carpenters, gardeners, inventors — but somebody: to become successful, famous, powerful; to become something that will bring, not quiet self-fulfilment, but self-glorification, self-expansion. You are looking at people who have lost their innocence because they have chosen not to be themselves but to promote themselves, to show off, even if it be only in their own eyes.

Look at your daily life. Is there a single thought, word or action untainted by the desire to become somebody, even if all you seek to become is a spiritual success or a saint unknown to anyone except yourself?

The child, like the innocent animal, surrenders to its nature to be and become quite simply what it is.

Adults who have preserved their innocence also surrender like the child to the impulse of Nature or Destiny without a thought to become somebody or to impress others; but, unlike the child, they rely, not on instinct, but on ceaseless awareness of everything in them and around them; that awareness shields them from evil and brings about the growth that was intended for them by Nature, not designed by their ambitious egos.

III.   Here is another way that grown-ups corrupt the

innocence of childhood: they teach the child to imitate someone. The moment you make the child a carbon copy you stamp out the spark of originality with which it came into the world. The moment you choose to become like someone else however great or holy, you have prostituted your being.

> Think sadly of the divine spark of uniqueness that lies within you, buried under layers of fear. The fear that you will be ridiculed or rejected if you dare to be yourself and refuse to conform mechanically in the way you dress and act and think. See how you conform not only in your actions and thoughts but even in your reactions, your emotions, your attitudes, your values. You dare not break out of this prostitution and reclaim your original innocence. This is the price you pay for the passport of acceptance by your society or organization. So you enter the world of the crooked and the controlled and are exiled from the kingdom that belongs to the innocence of childhood.

IV. One final subtle way you destroy your innocence is when you compete and compare yourself with others. When you do that you exchange your simplicity for the ambition of wanting to be as good as someone else or even better.

> Think of this: the reason why the child is able to preserve its innocence and live like the rest of creation in the bliss of the kingdom is that it has not been sucked into what we call the world — that region of darkness inhabited by grown-ups whose lives are spent not in living but in courting applause and admiration; not in blissfully being themselves but in neurotically comparing and competing, striving for those empty things called success and fame even if they can be attained only at

the expense of defeating, humiliating, destroying their neighbours.

V.   If you allow yourself to really feel the pains of this hell on earth, the utter emptiness it brings, you might experience within you a revolt, a disgust so powerful that it will shatter the chains of dependence and deceit that have been forged around your soul and you will break loose into the kingdom of innocence where mystics and children dwell.

MEDITATION 18

QUALITIES OF LOVE

This is my commandment, that you love one another as I have loved you. Jn. 15, 12

What is love? Take a look at a rose. Is it possible for the rose to say, "I shall offer my fragrance to good people and withhold it from bad people?" Or can you imagine a lamp that withholds its rays from a wicked person who seeks to walk in its light? It could only do that by ceasing to be a lamp.

And observe how helplessly and indiscriminately a tree gives its shade to everyone, good and bad, young and old, high and low; to animals and humans and every living creature even to the one who seeks to cut it down.

I. *This is the first quality of love: its indiscriminate character.*

That is why we are exhorted to be like God, "who makes his sun to shine on good and bad alike and makes his rain to fall on saints and sinners alike; so you must be all goodness as your heavenly Father is all goodness."

A.   Contemplate in astonishment the sheer goodness of the rose, the lamp, the tree, for there you have an image of what love is all about.

How does one attain this quality of love? Anything you do will only make it forced, cultivated and therefore phony, for love cannot be forced. There is nothing you can do. But there is something you can drop.

B.   Observe the marvellous change that comes over you the moment you stop seeing people as good and bad, as saints and sinners and begin to see them as unaware and ignorant.

> You must drop your false belief that people can sin in awareness. No one can sin in the light of awareness. Sin occurs, not as we mistakenly think, in malice but in ignorance. "Father, forgive them for they do not know what they are doing." To see this is to acquire the indiscriminate quality one so admires in the rose, the lamp and the tree.

II. And here is a *second quality of love — ts gratuitousness.* Like the tree, the rose, the lamp, it gives and asks for nothing in return.

> How we despise the man whose choice of his wife is determined not by any quality she may have but by the amount of money she will bring as dowry. Such a man, we rightly say, loves not the woman but the financial benefit she brings him. But is your own love any different when you seek the company of those who bring you emotional gratification and avoid those who don't; when you are positively disposed towards people who give you what you want and live up to your expectations and are negative or indifferent towards those who don't?

Here too there is only one thing that you need do to

acquire this quality of gratuitousness that characterizes love. You can open your eyes and see. Just seeing, just exposing your so-called love for what it really is, a camouflage for selfishness and greed, is a major step towards arriving at this second quality of love.

III.   The *third quality of love is its unself-consciousness.* Love so enjoys the loving that it is blissfully unaware of itself.

> The way the lamp is busy shining with no thought of whether it is benefitting others or not. The way a rose gives out its fragrance simply because there is nothing else it can do, whether there is someone to enjoy the fragrance or not. The way the tree offers its shade.

The light, the fragrance and the shade are not produced at the approach of persons and turned off when there is no one there. These things, like love, exist independently of persons. Love simply is, it has no object. They simply are, regardless of whether someone will benefit from them or not. So they have no consciousness of any merit or of doing good. Their left hand has no consciousness of what their right hand does. "Lord when did we see you hungry or thirsty and help you?"

IV.   The *final quality of love is its freedom.* The moment coercion or control or conflict enter, love dies. Think how the rose, the tree, the lamp leave you completely free.

> The tree will make no effort to drag you into its shade if you are in danger of a sunstroke. The lamp will not force its light on you lest you stumble in the dark.

A.   Think for a while of all the coercion and control that you submit to on the part of others when you so anxiously live up to their expectations in order to buy their love and approval or because you fear you will lose them. Each time you submit to this control and this coercion you destroy the capacity to love which is your very nature, for you cannot but do to others what you allow others to do to you.

B.   Contemplate, then, all the control and coercion in your life and hopefully this contemplation alone will cause them to drop. The moment they drop, freedom will arise. And freedom is just another word for love.

MEDITATION 19

RELIEF & ATTACHMENT : OBSTACLES TO LOVE

No one who puts his hand to the plough and looks back is fit for the kingdom of God.   *Lk. 9, 62*

God's kingdom is love. What does it mean to love? It means to be sensitive to life, to things, to persons, to feel for everything and everyone to the exclusion of nothing and no one.

For exclusion can only be achieved through a hardening of oneself, through closing one's doors. And the moment there is a hardening, sensitivity dies. It won't be hard for you to find examples of this kind of sensitivity in your life.

Have you ever stopped to remove a stone or a nail from the road lest someone came to harm? It does not matter that you will never know the person who will benefit from this gesture and you will receive no reward or recognition. You just do it from a feeling of benevolence and kindness.

Or have you felt pained at the wanton destruction in another part of the world, of a forest that you will never see and never benefit from? Have you gone to some trouble to help a stranger find his way though you do not know and will never meet this person again, purely from a good-heartedness that you feel within you?

In these and so many other moments, love came to the surface in your life signalling that it was there within you waiting to be released.

How can you come to possess this kind of love? You cannot, because it is already there within you. All you have to do is remove the blocks you place to sensitivity and it would surface.

The blocks to sensitivity are two; Belief and Attachment.

I.   *Belief* — as soon as you have a belief you have come to a conclusion about a person or situation or thing. You have now become fixed and have dropped your sensitivity. You are prejudiced and will see the person from the eye of that prejudice. In other words, you will cease to see this person again. And how can you be sensitive to someone you do not even see?

Take just one or two of your acquaintances and list the many positive or negative conclusions you have arrived at and on the basis of which you relate to her/him. The moment you say so-and-so is wise or is cruel or defensive or loving or whatever, you have hardened your perception and become prejudiced and ceased to perceive this person moment by moment, somewhat like a pilot who operates today with last week's weather report.

Take a hard look at these beliefs, for the mere realization that they are beliefs, conclusions, prejudices, not reflections of reality, will cause them to drop.

II.   *Attachment*—how is an attachment formed?

1.   First comes the contact with something that gives you pleasure: a car, an attractively advertised modern appliance, a word of praise, a person's company.

2.   Then comes the desire to hold on to it, to repeat the gratifying sensation that this thing or person caused you.

3.   Finally comes the conviction that you will not be happy without this person or thing, for you have equated the pleasure it brings you with happiness.

> You now have a full blown attachment; and with it comes an inevitable exclusion of other things, an insensitivity to anything that isn't part of your attachment.

Each time you leave the object of your attachment, you leave your heart there, so you cannot invest it in the next place you go to.

> The symphony of life moves on but you keep looking back, clinging to a few bars of the melody, blocking your ears to the rest of the music thereby producing disharmony and conflict between what life is offering you and what you are clinging to.

Then comes the tension and anxiety which are the very death of love and the joyful freedom that love brings. For love and freedom are only found when one enjoys each note as it arises, then allows it to go, so as to be fully receptive to the notes that follow.

How does one drop an attachment?

> People try to do this through renunciation. But to renounce some bars of the music, to blot them out of one's consciousness creates exactly the type of violence, conflict and insensitivity that clinging does. Once again you have hardened yourself.

A.   The secret is to renounce nothing, cling to nothing, enjoy everything and allow it to pass, to flow. How? Through many hours of observing the rottenness, the corrupt nature of an attachment.

You generally concentrate on the thrill, the flash of pleasure that it brings.

B.   But contemplate the anxiety, the pain, the lack of freedom; simultaneously contemplate the joy, the peace and freedom that are yours each time an attachment drops.

C.   Then you will stop looking back and allow yourself to be enchanted by the music of the present moment.

D.   Finally take a look at this society we live in — rotten to the core, infected as it is with attachments.

For if anyone is attached to power, money, property, to fame and success; if anyone seeks these things as if their happiness depended on them, they will be considered productive members of society, dynamic and hardworking. In other words, if they pursue these things with a driving ambition that destroys the symphony of their life and makes them hard and cold and insensitive to others and to themselves, society will look upon them as dependable citizens, and their relatives and friends will be proud of the status that they have achieved.

How many so-called respectable people do you know who have retained the gentle sensitivity of love that only un-attachment can offer? If you contemplate this long enough, you will experience a disgust so deep that you will instinctively fling every attachment away as you would a serpent that has settled on you. You will revolt and break loose from this putrid culture that is based on acquisitiveness and attachment, on anxiety and greed and on the hardness and insensitivity of non-love.

MEDITATION 20

LOVING IS SEEING

But I say to you that hear, Love your enemies, do
good to those who hate you.   Lk. 6, 27

When you are in love you find yourself looking at
everyone with new eyes; you become generous,
forgiving, kind-hearted, where before you might
have been hard, and mean. Inevitably, people begin
reacting to you in the same way and soon you find
yourself living in a loving world that you yourself
have created.

> Or think of the time you were in a bad mood
> and found yourself becoming irritable, mean,
> suspicious, even paranoid. The next thing you
> knew, everyone was reacting to you in a
> negative way and you found yourself living in
> a hostile world created by your head and your
> emotions.

How could you go about creating a happy, loving,
peaceful world? By learning a simple, beautiful, but
painful art called the art of looking. This is how you
do it:

1. Every time you find yourself irritated or angry with
    someone, the one to look at is not that person but

yourself. The question to ask is not, `What's wrong with this person', but `What does this irritation tell me about myself?'.

> Do this right now. Think of some irritating person you know and say this painful but liberating sentence to yourself : "The cause of my irritation is not in this person but in me." Having said that, begin the task of finding out how you are causing the irritation.

2. Initially look into the very real possibility that the reason why this person's defects or so called defects annoy you, is that you have them yourself. But you have repressed them and so are projecting them unconsciously into the other.

> This is almost always true but hardly anyone recognizes it. So search for this person's defects in your own heart and in your unconscious mind, and your annoyance will turn to gratitude that his or her behaviour has led you to self-discovery.

3. Here is something else worth looking at: Can it be that you are annoyed at what this person says or does because those words and behaviour are pointing out to something in your life and in yourself that you are refusing to see?

> Think how irritated people become with the mystic and the prophet who look far from mystical or prophetical when we are challenged by their words or their life.

4. Another thing is also clear: you become irritated with this person because he/she is not living up to the expectations that have been programmed into you.

> May be you have a right to demand that he or she live up to your programming, as for instance, when he or she is cruel or unjust,

but then stop to consider this. If you seek to change this person or to stop this person's behaviour, will you not be more effective if you were not irritated?

Irritation will only cloud your perception and make your action less effective.

Everyone knows that when a sportsman or a boxer loses his temper, the quality of his play goes down because it becomes un-coordinated through passion and anger. In most cases, however, you have no right to demand that this person live up to your expectations; someone else in your place would be exposed to this behaviour and would experience no annoyance at all. Just contemplate this truth and your irritation will vanish.

How foolish of you to demand that someone else live up to standards and norms that your parents programmed into you?

5.   And here is a final truth for you to consider: Given the background, the life experience, and the unawareness of this person, he cannot help behaving the way he does. It has been so well said that to understand all is to forgive all.

If you really understood this person you would see him as crippled and not blameworthy, and your irritation would instantly cease.

And the next thing you know you will be treating him/her with love, and he/she is responding with love and you find yourself living in a loving world which you have yourself created.

MEDITATION 21

BECOMING FEARLESS AND FREE

The pharisees said to his disciples, 'Why does your teacher eat with tax collectors and sinners?'
Mt. 9, 11

I. If you wish to get in touch with the reality of a thing, the first thing you must understand is that every idea distorts reality and is a barrier to seeing reality. The idea is not the reality, the idea "wine" is not wine, the idea "woman" is not this woman.

If I really want to get in touch with the reality of this woman I must put aside my idea of "woman" or Indian and experience her in her "thisness", her concreteness, her uniqueness. Unfortunately most people most of the time do not take the trouble to see things like this in their uniqueness; they just see the words or the ideas; they never look with the eyes of a child at this concrete, unique, fluffy, alive thing that is moving out there in front of them. They only see a sparrow, they never see the wondrous marvel of this unique human being here in front of them; they only see an Indian peasant woman.

The idea therefore is a barrier to the perception of reality.

II. There is yet another barrier to the perception of reality — the judgment. This thing or person is good or bad, ugly or beautiful.

It is barrier enough to have the idea of Indian or woman or peasant when I look at this concrete individual. But now I add a judgment and I say, "She is good, or she is bad, she is attractive and beautiful or she is unattractive and ugly." That further prevents me from seeing her because she is neither good or bad. She is 'she' in all her uniqueness. The crocodile and the tiger are neither good nor bad, they are crocodile and tiger. Good and bad are in relation to something outside them. In as much as they suit my purpose or please my eyes, or help me, or threaten me, I call them good or bad.

Now think of yourself when you were called good or attractive or beautiful by someone. Either you hardened yourself because you really thought you were ugly and you said to yourself, "If you really knew me as I am you would not call me beautiful." Or you opened yourself to the words of that person and you really thought that you were beautiful and you allowed yourself to be thrilled at the compliment. In both cases you were wrong, because you are neither beautiful nor ugly. You are You.

If you get caught up in the judgments of people around you, you are eating the fruit of tension and insecurity and anxiety, because when today they call you beautiful and you are elated, tomorrow they will call you ugly and you will be depressed.

Therefore, the proper and accurate response when someone calls you beautiful is to say, "This person given his present perception and mood sees me as beautiful, but that does not say anything about me.

> Someone else in his place and depending on his background and mood and perception will see me as ugly, But that again says nothing about me."

> How easily we are taken in by the judgment of other people and then form an image of ourselves based on this judgment.

III.   In order to be truly liberated you need to listen to the so-called good and bad things that they tell you, but to feel no emotion at the feedback any more than a computer does when data is fed into it. Because what they say about you reveals more about them than about you.

> As a matter of fact you also have to be aware of the judgments that you make about yourself, because even those are generally based on the value systems that you picked up from the people around you. If you judge, condemn, approve, do you ever see reality? If you look at anything through the eye of judgment or approval or condemnation, is that not the major barrier to understanding and observing things as they are in themselves? Take the time when somebody told you that you are very special to him; if you accepted that compliment then you ate the fruit of tension. Why do you want to be special to someone and to submit to that kind of approval and judgment? Why not just be content to be you?

When someone tells you how special you are, all that you can accurately say is: "This person given his particular taste and needs, desires, appetites and projections has a special desire for me, but that says nothing about me as a person. Someone else will find me quite unspecial and that too says nothing about me as a person. "

So the moment you accept that compliment and you allow yourself to enjoy it, you will give control of yourself to that person. You will go to great lengths in order to continue to be special to this person. You will be in constant fear lest he meets someone who will become special to him and thus you will be dislodged from the special position you occupy in his life.

And you will be constantly dancing to his tunes, living up to his expectations, and in doing so you will have lost your freedom. You have made yourself dependent on him for your happiness, for you have made your happiness depend on his judgment of you.

Then you can make things worse by beginning to search for other people who will tell you that you are special to them and you invest so much time and energy in making sure that they never lose this image they have of you. What a wearisome way to live!

Suddenly fear comes into your life, fear that the image will be destroyed, and if what you seek is fearlessness and freedom, you must let go of this. How? By refusing to take anybody seriously when they tell you how special you are.

The words — "You are special to me" simply say something about my present mood regarding you, my taste, my present state of mind and development. It says nothing else. So accept that as a fact and do not rejoice in it. What you may rejoice in is my company and not my compliment. What you may enjoy is my present interaction with you, not my praise.

And if you are wise, you will urge me to find many other special people so that you are never tempted to hold on to this image that I have of you. It is not my image of you that you enjoy because you are ceaselessly aware that my image of you can change so easily.

So what you enjoy is the present moment, because if you enjoy the image that I have of you, I will control you and you will be afraid to be yourself lest you hurt me. You will be afraid to tell me the truth, to do or say anything that would damage the image that I have of you.

Apply this now to every image that people have of you and they tell you that you are a genius or wise or good or holy, and you enjoy that compliment and in that minute you lose your freedom; because now you will be constantly striving to retain that opinion. You will fear to make mistakes, to be yourself, to do or say anything that will spoil the image.

You have lost the freedom to make a fool of yourself, to be laughed at and to be ridiculed, to do and say whatever feels right to you rather than what fits in with the image others have of you.

How does one break this? Through many patient hours of study, awareness, observation, of what this silly image brings you. It gives you a thrill combined with so much insecurity and unfreedom and suffering. If you were to see this clearly you would lose your appetite to be special to anyone, or to be highly regarded by anyone.

You would move about with sinners or bad characters and do and say as you please, regardless of what people think of you.

You would become like the birds and flowers that are so totally unselfconscious, too busy with the task of living to care one little bit about what others think of them, about whether they are special to others or not. And at last, you will have become fearless and free.

MEDITATION 22

THE INGREDIENTS OF LOVE

*Blessed are those servants whom the master finds
awake when he comes.*   *Lk. 12, 37*

Everywhere in the world people are in search of love,
for everyone is convinced that love alone can save
the world, love alone can make life meaningful and
worth living.

> But how very few understand what love really
> is, and how it arises in the human heart. It is
> so frequently equated with good feelings
> towards others, with benevolence or
> non-violence or service. But these things in
> themselves are not love.

Love springs from awareness. It is only in as much
as you see someone as he or she really is here and
now and not as they are in your memory or your
desire or in your imagination or projection that you
can truly love them.

> Otherwise it is not the person that you love
> but the idea that you have formed of this
> person, or this person as the object of your
> desire not as he or she is in themselves.

I.   Therefore the first act of love is to see this person or this object, this reality as it truly is. And this involves the enormous discipline of dropping your desires, your prejudices, your memories, your projections, your selective way of looking, a discipline so great that most people would rather plunge headlong into good actions and service than submit to the burning fire of this asceticism.

> When you set out to serve someone whom you have not taken the trouble to see, are you meeting that person's need or your own? So the first ingredient of love is to really see the other.

II.   The second ingredient is equally important to see yourself, to ruthlessly flash the light of awareness on your motives, your emotions, your needs, your dishonest, your self-seeking, your tendency to control and manipulate. This means calling things by their name, no matter how painful the discovery and the consequences.

> If you achieve this kind of awareness of the other and yourself, you will know what love is. For you will have attained a mind and a heart that is alert, vigilant, clear, sensitive, a clarity of perception, a sensitivity that will draw out of you an accurate, appropriate response to every situation at every moment. Sometimes you will be irresistibly impelled into action, at others you will be held back and restrained. You will sometimes be made to ignore others and sometimes give them the attention they seek. At times you will be gentle and yielding, at others hard, uncompromising, assertive, even violent.

For the love that is born of sensitivity takes many unexpected forms and it responds not to prefabricated guidelines and principles but to present, concrete reality. When you first experience this kind of sensitivity you are likely to experience terror. For all your defences will be torn down, your dishonesty exposed, the protected walls around you burnt.

> Think of the terror that comes to a rich man when he sets out to really see the pitiful condition of the poor, to a power hungry dictator when he really looks at the plight of the people he oppresses, to a fanatic, a bigot, when he really sees the falsehood of his convictions when they do not fit the facts. The terror that comes to the romantic lover when he decides to really see that what he loves is not his beloved but his image of her.

That is why the most painful act the human being can perform, the act that he dreads the most is the act of seeing. It is in that act of seeing that love is born, or rather more accurately, that act of seeing is Love.

Once you begin to see, your sensitivity will drive you to the awareness, not just of the things that you choose to see but of everything else as well.

> Your poor ego will try desperately to blunt that sensitivity because its defences are being stripped away and it is left with no protection and nothing to cling to.

If you ever allow yourself to see, it will be the death of you. And that is why love is so terrifying, for to love is to see and to see is to die. But it is also the most delightful, exhilarating experience in the whole world. For in the death of the ego is freedom, peace, serenity, joy.

If it is love that you truly desire then set out at once on the task of seeing.

> Take it seriously and look at someone you dislike and really see your prejudice. Look at

someone you cling to or something you cling to and really see the suffering, the futility, the unfreedom of clinging and look long and lovingly at human faces and human behaviour. Take some time out to gaze in wonder at nature, the flight of a bird, a flower in bloom, the dry leaf crumbling to dust, the flow of a river, the rising of the moon, a silhouette of a mountain against the sky. And as you do this the hard, protective shell around your heart will soften and melt and your heart will come alive in sensitivity and responsiveness. The darkness in your eyes will be dispelled and your vision will become clear and penetrating, and you will know at last what love is.

MEDITATION 23

SEEING IS A PREREQUISITE FOR LIVING

And after he had dismissed the crowds, he went up on the mountain by himself to pray.

Mt. 14, 23

Has it ever occurred to you that you can only love when you are alone.

What does it mean to love?

It means to see a person, a thing, a situation, as it really is and not as you imagine it to be, and to give it the response it deserves. You can not love what you do not even see.

> And what prevents you from seeing? Your concepts, your categories, your prejudices and projections, your needs and attachments, the labels you have drawn from your conditioning and from your past experiences.

Seeing is the most arduous thing a human being can undertake. For it calls for a disciplined, alert mind, whereas most people would much rather lapse into mental laziness than take the trouble to see each person and thing anew in present moment freshness.

To drop your conditioning in order to see is arduous enough. But seeing calls for something more painful still. The dropping of the control that society exercises over you; a control whose tentacles have penetrated to the very roots of your being, so that to drop it is to tear yourself apart.

> If you wish to understand this, think of a little child that is given a taste for drugs. As the drug penetrates the body of the child, it becomes addicted and its whole being cries out for the drug. To be without the drug is so unbearable a torment that it seems preferable to die.

> Now this is exactly what society did to you when you were a child. You were not allowed to enjoy the solid, nutritious food of life: work and play and the company of people and the pleasures of the senses and the mind. You were given a taste for the drug called Approval, Appreciation, Attention, the drug called Success, Prestige, Power. Having got a taste for these things, you became addicted and began to dread their loss. You felt terror at the prospect of failure, of mistakes, of the criticism of others. So you became cravenly dependent on people and lost your freedom.

Others now have the power to make you happy or miserable. And much as you now hate the suffering this involves, you find yourself completely helpless. There is never a minute when, consciously or unconsciously, you are not attuned to the reaction of others, marching to the drum of their demands. When you are ignored or disapproved of, you experience a loneliness so unbearable that you crawl back to people to beg for the comfort known as Support, Encouragement, Reassurance. To live with people in this state involves never ending tension; but to live without them brings the agony of loneliness.

You have lost your capacity to see them clearly as they are and to respond to them accurately because mostly your perception of them is clouded by your need to get your drug.

The consequence of all this is terrifying and inescapable: You have become incapable of loving anyone or anything. If you wish to love you must learn to see again.

And if you wish to see, you must give up your drug. You must tear away from your being the roots of society that have penetrated to the marrow. You must drop out. Externally everything will go on as before, you will continue to be in the world, but no longer of it. And in your heart you will now be free at last and utterly alone. It is only in this aloneness, this utter solitude, that dependence and desire will die, and the capacity to love is born. For one no longer sees others as means to satisfy one's addiction.

Only someone who has attempted this knows the terror of the process. It is like inviting yourself to die. It is like asking the poor drug addict to give up the only happiness he has known and to replace it with a taste for bread and fruit and the clean, fresh morning air and the sweetness of the water from the mountain stream, while he is struggling to cope with his withdrawal symptoms and with the emptiness that he experiences within himself now that his drug has gone. To his fevered mind nothing can fill the emptiness except his drug.

Can you imagine a life in which you refuse to enjoy a single word of approval and appreciation, or to lean on someone's arm; in which you depend on no one emotionally, so no one has the power to make you happy or miserable any more; you refuse to need any particular person, or to be special to anyone, or to call anyone your own? Even the birds of the air have their nests and the foxes their holes, but you will have nowhere to rest your head in your journey through life.

If you ever get to this state you will at last know what it means to see with a vision that is clear and unclouded by fear or desire. And you will know what it means to love. But to come to this land of love you have to pass through the pains of death. For to love persons is to have died to the need for persons and to be utterly alone.

How would you ever get there?

1.   By ceaseless awareness,

2.   With the infinite patience and compassion that you would have for a drug addict.

3.   It will also help you to undertake activities that you can do with your whole being, activities that you so much love to do, that while you are engaged in them, success or recognition or approval simply do not mean a thing to you.

4.   It will help too if you return to Nature: send the crowds away and go up into the mountain and silently commune with trees and flowers and animals and birds, with sea and sky and clouds and stars. Then you will know that your heart has brought you into the vast desert of solitude. There is no one there by your side, absolutely no one.

At first it will seem unbearable, but that is only because you are unaccustomed to aloneness. But if you manage to stay there for a while the desert will suddenly blossom into Love. Your heart will burst into song. And it will be springtime forever.

MEDITATION 24

CONTEMPLATION LEADS TO TRANSFORMATION

Judge not, that you be not judged. Mt. 7:1

It is a sobering thought that the finest act of love you can perform is not an act of service but an act of contemplation, of seeing.

When you serve people, you help, support, comfort, alleviate pain. When you see them in their inner beauty and goodness, you transform and create.

I. Think of some of the people you like and are drawn to you.

Now attempt to look at each of them as if you were seeing them for the first time, not allowing yourself to be influenced by your past knowledge or experience of them, whether good or bad.

Look for things in them that you may have missed because of familiarity, for familiarity breeds staleness, blindness and boredom. You cannot love what you cannot see afresh. You cannot love what you are not constantly discovering anew.

II. Having done this move on now to people you dislike.

First observe what is it in them that you dislike, study their defects impartially and with detachment.

> That means you cannot use labels like proud, lazy, selfish, arrogant. The label is an act of mental laziness, for it is easy to stick a label onto someone. It is difficult and challenging to see this person in his/her uniqueness.

You must study those defects clinically, that means, you must first make sure of your objectivity.

A.   Consider the possibility that what you see as a defect in them, may not be a defect at all, but really something that your upbringing and conditioning have led you to dislike.

B.   If after this you still see a defect there, understand that the origin of the defect lies in childhood experiences, past conditionings, faulty thinking and perception; and above all in unawareness, not in malice.

> As you do this, your attitude will change into love and forgiveness, for to study, to observe, to understand is to forgive.

C.   Having made this study of defects, now search for the treasures buried in this person that your dislike prevented you from seeing before.

D.   And as you do this, observe any change of attitude or feeling that comes over you, for your dislike had clouded the vision and prevented you from seeing.

> You can now move on to each of the persons you live and work with, observing how each of them becomes transformed in your eyes when you look at them in this way.

In seeing them thus it is an infinitely more loving gift that you offer them than any act of service. For in doing this, you have transformed them, you have created them in your heart and, given a certain amount of contact between you and them they will be transformed in reality too.

III. Now make this same gift to yourself. If you have been able to do it for others that should be fairly easy. Follow the same procedure: no defect, no neuroses is judged or condemned. You have not judged others, you will be amazed now that you yourself are not being judged.

Those defects are probed, studied, analysed, for a better understanding that leads to love and forgiveness, and you will discover to your joy that you are being transformed by this strangely loving attitude that arises within you towards this thing you call yourself. An attitude that arises within you and moves out through you to every living creature.

MEDITATION 25

BE VIOLENT WITH YOUR ATTACHMENTS

And if your hand causes you to sin, cut it off, it is better to enter life maimed than with two hands to go to hell.... And if your eye causes you to sin, pluck it out; it is better for you to enter the kingdom of God with one eye than with two eyes to be thrown into hell. Mk. 9, 43 ff

When you deal with blind people it dawns on you that they are attuned to realities that you have no idea of. Their sensitivity to the world of touch and smell and taste and sound is such, as to make the rest of us seem like dull clods. We pity persons who have lost their sight but rarely take into account the enrichment that their other senses offer them. It is a pity that those riches are bought at the heavy price of blindness and it is quite conceivable that we could be as alive and finely attuned to the world as blind people are without the loss of our eyes.

It is not possible, not even conceivable, that you would ever awaken to the world of love unless you pluck out, chop off, those parts of your psychological being that are called Attachments.

If you refuse to do this, you will miss the experience of Love, you miss the only thing that gives meaning to human existence. For love is the passport to abiding joy and peace and freedom. There is only one thing that blocks out entry into that world and the name of that thing is Attachment.

> It is produced by the lusting eye that excites craving within the heart and by the grasping hand that reaches out to hold, possess and make one's own, and refuses to let go. It is this eye that must be gouged out, this hand that must be cut off if Love is to be born. With those mutilated stumps for hands you can grasp nothing any more. With those empty sockets for eyes you suddenly become sensitive to realities whose existence you have never suspected.

Now at last you can love. Till now all you had was certain good heartedness and benevolence, a sympathy and concern for others, which you mistakenly took for Love but has as little in common with Love, as a flickering candle flame has with the light of the sun.

What is Love? It is a sensitivity to every portion of reality within you and without, together with a whole-hearted response to that reality.

> Sometimes you will embrace that reality, sometimes you will attack it, sometimes you will ignore it, and at others you will give it your fullest attention, but always you will respond not from need but from sensitivity.

And what is an attachment? A need, a clinging that blunts your sensitivity, a drug that clouds your perception. That is why as long as you have the slightest attachment for anything or any person, Love cannot be born.

For Love is sensitivity, and sensitivity that is impaired even in the slightest degree is sensitivity destroyed. Just as the malfunctioning of one essential piece of a radar set distorts reception, an attackment distorts your response to what you perceive.

There is no such thing as defective love, or deficient love, or partial love. Love like sensitivity either is in all its fullness or it simply is not. You either have it whole, or you have it not.

So it is only when attachments disappear that one enters the boundless realm of spiritual freedom called Love. One is now released to see and to respond. But you must not confound this freedom with the indifference of those who have never passed through the stage of attachment.

How could you pluck out an eye or amputate a hand that you do not have? This indifference that so many people mistake for love (because they are attached to no one, they think that they love everyone) is not sensitivity, but a hardening of the heart that has come about from rejection or disillusionment or the practice of renunciation.

No, one must brave the stormy seas of attachments if one has to arrive at the land of love.

Some people, never having set sail have convinced themselves that they have arrived. One must be able-bodied and clear-sighted before the sword can do its work and the world of love can arise in one's awareness; and make no mistake, this is only achieved through violence. It is only the violent who carry off the kingdom.

Why the violence? Because left to its own devices life

would never produce love, it would only lead you to
attraction, from attraction to pleasure, then to
attachment, to satisfaction, which finally leads to
wearisomeness and boredom. Then comes a
plateau. Then once again the weary cycle:
attraction, pleasure, attachment, fulfillment,
satisfaction, boredom. All of this mixed with the
anxieties, the jealousies, the possessiveness, the
sorrow, the pain, that makes the cycle a roller
coaster.

> When you have gone repeatedly round and
> round the cycle, a time finally comes when
> you have had enough and want to call a halt
> to the whole process. And if you are lucky
> enough not to run into something or someone
> else that catches your eye, you will have at
> least attained a fragile peace. That is the most
> that life can give you; and you can mistakenly
> equate this state with freedom and you die
> without ever having known what it means to
> be really free and to love.

No. if you wish to break out of the cycle and into the
world of love, you must strike while the attachment
is alive and raw, not when you have outgrown it.
And you must strike not with the sword of
renunciation, for that kind of mutilation only
hardens, but with the sword of awareness.

What must you be aware of? Three things:

I.   First you must see the suffering that this drug is
       causing you, the ups and downs, the thrills, the
       anxieties and disappointments, the boredom to
       which it must inevitably lead.

II.   Second, you must realize what this drug is cheating
       you out of, namely, the freedom to love and to enjoy
       every minute and every thing in life.

III.   Third, you must understand how, because of your
       addiction and your programming, you have invested

the object of your attachment with a beauty and a value it simply does not have: what you are so enamoured of is in your head, not in your beloved person or thing. See this and the sword of awareness breaks the spell.

It is commonly held that it is only when you feel deeply loved yourself, that you are able to go out in love to others. This is not true. A man in love, does indeed go out to the world not in love but in euphoria. For him the world takes on an unreal, rosy hue, which it loses the moment the euphoria dies. His so called love is generated not by his clear perception of reality but by the conviction, true or false, that he is loved by someone — a conviction that is dangerously fragile, because it is founded on the unreliable, changeable people, who he believes love him. And who can at any moment pull the switch and turn off his euphoria. No wonder those who walk this path never really lose their insecurity.

(When you go out to the world because of the love that someone else has for you, you are all aglow not with your perception of reality but with the love that you have received from someone else, someone else controls the switch and when it is switched off the glow fades away.)

As you use the sword of awareness to move from attachment into love, there is one thing you must keep in mind: Don't be harsh or impatient, or hating of yourself. How can love grow out of such attitudes? But rather hold on to the compassion and the matter-of-factness with which the surgeon plies his knife. Then you may find yourself in the marvellous condition of loving the object of your attachment and enjoying it even more than before, but simultaneously enjoying every other thing, and every other person just as much.

That is the litmus test for finding out if what you have is love. Far from becoming indifferent, you now enjoy everything, and everyone just as much as you did the object of your attachment. Only now there are no more thrills and therefore no more suffering and suspense. In fact you could be said to be enjoying everything and enjoying nothing. Because you have made the great discovery that what you are enjoying on the occasion of each thing and person is something within yourself.

The orchestra is within you and you carry it with you wherever you go. The things and people outside you merely determine what particular melody the orchestra will play. And when there is no one or nothing that has your attention, the orchestra will play a music of its own; it needs no outside stimulation. You now carry in your heart a happiness that nothing outside of you can put there, and nothing can take away.

Here then is the other test of love.

You are happy for no reason that you know.

Does this love last? There is no guarantee that it does. For while love cannot be partial it can be of temporary duration. It comes and goes in the measure that your mind is awake and aware or has gone off to sleep again. But this much is certain, once you have had even a fleeting taste of this thing called Love, you will know that no price is too high, no sacrifice too great, not even the loss of one's eyes, nor the amputations of one's hand, if you can have in exchange the only thing in the world that makes your life worthwhile.

GROWING THROUGH PAINFUL EVENTS

*Was it not necessary that the Christ should suffer
these things and enter into his glory? Lk. 24, 26*

Think of some of the painful events in your
life. For how many of them are you grateful
today, because thanks to them you changed
and grew.

Here is a simple truth of life that most people never
discover. Happy events make life delightful but they
do not lead to self-discovery and growth and
freedom. That privilege is reserved to the things and
persons and situations that cause us pain.

Every painful event contains in itself a seed of
growth and liberation. In the light of this truth
return to your life now and take a look at one or
another of the events that you are not grateful for,
and see if you can discover the potential for growth
that they contain which you were unaware of and
therefore failed to benefit from. Now think of some
recent event that caused you pain, that produced
negative feelings in you.

Whoever or whatever caused those feelings
was your Teacher, because they revealed so

much to you about yourself that you probably did not know. And they offered you an invitation and a challenge to self-understanding, self-discovery, and therefore to growth and life and freedom.

I. Try it out now, identify the negative feeling that this event aroused in you. Was it anxiety or insecurity, jealousy or anger or guilt. What does that emotion say to you about yourself, your values, your way of perceiving the world and life, and above all your programming and conditioning.

If you succeed in discovering this, you will drop some illusion you have clung to till now, or you will change a distorted perception or correct a false belief or learn to distance yourself from your suffering, as you realize that it was caused by your programming and not by reality; and you will suddenly find that you are full of gratitude for those negative feelings and to that person or event that caused them.

II. Now take this one step further. Look at everything that you think and feel and say and do that you do not like in yourself. Your negative emotions, your defects, your handicaps, your errors, your attachments and neuroses and hangups and yes, even your sins. Can you see everyone of them as a necessary part of your development, holding out a promise of growth and grace for you and others, that would never have been there except for this thing that you so disliked.

And if you have caused pain and negative feelings to others, were you not at that moment a teacher to them, an instrument that offered them a seed for self-discovery and growth? Can you persist in this observation, in your observation till you see all of this as a happy fault, a necessary sin that brings so much good to you and to the world?

If you can, your heart will be flooded with peace and gratitude and love and acceptance of every single thing. And you will have discovered what people everywhere are searching for and never find. Namely, the fountain head of serenity and joy that hides in every human heart.

MEDITATION 27

FINDING THE JOY OF THE KINGDOM

I came to cast fire upon the earth; and would that it were already kindled!   *Lk. 12, 49*

If you want to know what it means to be happy; look at a flower, a bird, a child, they are perfect images of the kingdom. For they live from moment to moment in the eternal now with no past and no future. So they are spared the guilt and the anxiety that so torment human beings, and they are full of the sheer joy of living, taking delight not so much in persons or things as in life itself.

As long as your happiness is caused or sustained by something or someone outside of you, you are still in the land of the dead.

The day you are happy for no reason whatsoever, the day you find yourself taking delight in everything and in nothing, you will know that you have found the land of unending joy called the kingdom.

To find the kingdom is the easiest thing in the world, but also the most difficult. Easy because it is all around you and within you, and all you have to do is reach out and take possession of it. Difficult because if you wish to possess the kingdom you may possess nothing else.

That is, you must drop all inward leaning on any person or thing, withdrawing from them forever the power to thrill you, or excite you, or to give you a feeling of security or well being.

For this you first need to see with unflinching clarity this simple and shattering truth: Contrary to what your culture and religion have taught you, nothing, but absolutely nothing can make you happy.

The moment you see that, you will stop moving from one job to another, one friend to another, one place, one spiritual technique, one guru to another. None of these things can give you a single minute of happiness. They can only offer you a temporary thrill, a pleasure that initially grows in intensity, then turns into pain if you lose them, and into boredom if you keep them.

Think of the numberless persons and things that so excited you in the past. What happened? In every single instance they ended up by causing you suffering, or boredom, did they not? It is absolutely essential that you see this because till you do, there is no question of your ever finding the kingdom of joy. Mostly people are not prepared to see till they have suffered repeated disillusionment and sorrow. And even then only one in a million has the desire to see.

They just keep going at it, pathetically knocking at the door of other creatures, begging bowl in hand, craving affection and approval and guidance and power and honour and success. For they obstinately refuse to understand that happiness is not in these things.

If you search within your heart you will find something there that will make it possible for you to understand: a spark of disenchantment and discontent, which if fanned into flame will become a raging forest fire that will burn up the whole of the illusory world you are living in, thereby unveiling to your wondering eyes the kingdom that you have always lived in unsuspectingly.

Have you ever felt disgusted with life, sick at heart of constantly running away from fears and anxieties, weary of your begging rounds, exhausted from being dragged about helplessly by your attachments and addictions? Have you ever felt the utter meaninglessness of working for a degree, then finding a job, then settling down to a life of boredom; or, if you are an achiever, settling down to a life of emotional turmoil caused by the things that you are chasing after? If you have, and is there a single human being who hasn't, the divine flame of discontent has arisen within your heart. Now is the time to feed it before it gets stamped out by the routine chores of life.

Now is the Holy Season when you simply must find the time to get away and look at your life, allowing the flame to grow and grow as you look, refusing to let anything distract you from this task.

Now is the time to see that absolutely nothing outside of you can bring you lasting joy. But the moment you do that, you will notice that a fear arises in your heart. That fear that if you allow the discontent to be, it will turn into a raging passion that will grip you and cause you to revolt against everything that your culture and your religion, hold dear; against a whole way of thinking and feeling and perceiving the world that they have brainwashed you into accepting.

This devouring flame will cause you not just to rock the boat, but to burn the boat to ashes. Suddenly you will find yourself living in an altogether different world, infinitely removed from the world of the people around you, for everything that others hold dear, everything they are crying their hearts out for, honour, power, acceptance, approval, security, wealth, is seen for the stinking garbage that it is. It disgusts and nauseates. And everything others are forever running away from, holds no terrors for you any more. You have become serene and fearless and free, for you have stepped out of your illusory world and into the kingdom.

> Do not confound this divine discontent with the hopelessness and despair that sometimes drive people to madness and to suicide. That is not the mystical drive to life but the neurotic drive to self-destruction. Do not confound it with the whining of people who are forever complaining about everything. These people are not mystics but bores, merely agitating for improvement of prison conditions, whereas what they need to do is burst out of prison into freedom.

Most people, when they feel the stirring of this discontent within their hearts, either run away from it and drug themselves with the fevered pursuit of work and social life and friendship; or they channel the discontent into social work, literature, music, the so-called creative pursuits that make them settle for reform, when what is needed is revolt.

These people, even though they are full of activity, are not really alive at all: they are dead, content to live in the land of the dead.

The test that your discontent is divine is the fact that it has no trace of sadness or bitterness to it at all. On the contrary even though it often arouses fear within your heart, it is always accompanied by joy, the joy of the Kingdom.

And here is a parable of that kingdom: It is like a treasure lying buried in a field. The man who found it buried it again, and for sheer joy went and sold everything he had and bought that field. If you haven't found the treasure as yet, don't waste your time searching for it. It can be found but it may not be searched for. You don't have the slightest notion what the treasure is.

All you are familiar with is the drugged happiness of your present existence. So what would you search for? And where? No, search rather in your heart for the spark of discontent, and tend the flame till it becomes a conflagration and your world is burnt down to a heap of rubble.

Young or old, most of us are discontented merely because we want something — more knowledge, a better job, a finer car, a bigger salary. Our discontent is based upon our desire for "the more." It is only because we want something more that most of us are discontented. But I am not talking about that kind of discontent. It is the desire for 'the more' that prevents clear thinking, whereas if we are discontented, not because we want something, but without knowing what we want; if we are dissatisfied with our jobs, with making money, with seeking position and power, with tradition, with what we have and with what we might have; if we are dissatisfied, not with anything in particular but with everything, then I think we shall find that our discontent brings clarity. When we don't accept or follow, but question, investigate, penetrate, there is an insight out of which comes creativity, joy.

Mostly the discontent that you feel comes from not having enough of something — you are dissatisfied because you think you do not have enough money or power or success or fame or virtue or love, or holiness. This is not the discontent that leads to the joy of the kingdom. Its source is greed and ambition and its fruit is restlessness and frustration.

The day you are discontented, not because you want more of something but without knowing what it is you want; when you are sick at heart of everything that you have been pursuing so far, and you are sick of the pursuit itself, then your heart will attain a great clarity, an insight that will cause you mysteriously to delight in everything and in nothing.

MEDITATION 28

THE DISAPPEARANCE OF INSECURITY

Therefore I tell you, do not be anxious about your life... look at the birds of the air... consider the lilies of the field...　　　　　*Mt. 6, 25 ff.*

Everyone at some time or the other experiences feelings of what is known as insecurity.

> You feel insecure with the amount of money you have in the bank, or the amount of love you are getting from your friend or the type of educational background you have had. Or you have insecurity feelings regarding your health or your age or your physical appearance.

If you were asked the question, "What is it that makes you feel insecure?" you would almost certainly give the wrong answer.

> You might say, "I don't have enough of the love of a friend or I don't have the kind of academic training that I need," or some such thing.

In other words, you would point to some outside condition not realizing that insecurity feelings are not generated by anything outside of you, but only by your emotional programming, by something you are telling yourself in your head. If you change your programme, your insecurity feelings would vanish in a trice, even though everything in the outside world remained exactly as it was before.

One person feels quite secure with practically no money in the bank, another feels insecure even though he has millions. It isn't the amount of money but their programming that makes the difference. One person has no friends, yet feels perfectly secure in the love of people. Another feels insecure even in the most possessive and exclusive of relationships. Again the difference is in the programming.

If you wish to deal with your feelings of insecurity there are four facts that you must study well and understand.

I. *First*, it is futile to ease your insecurity feelings by trying to change things outside of you.

Your efforts may be successful, though mostly they are not. They may bring some relief, but the relief will be short-lived. So it is not worth the energy and time you spend in improving your physical appearance or making more money or getting further reassurances of love from your friends.

II. *Second*, this fact will lead you to tackle the problem where it really is, inside your head. Think of the people who in exactly the same condition that you find yourself in now, would not feel the slightest insecurity. There are such people. Therefore the problem lies not with reality outside of you but with you, in your programming.

III. *Third*, you must understand that this programming of yours was picked up from insecure people who, when you were very young and impressionable,

JAMES R. DOLAN, SJ, 1800 S. CLINTON AVE.
ROCHESTER, NY 14618 PH/FAX 585-244-2851
jrdolan@frontiernet.net

DEMELLO BOOKS
AWARENESS.................................. $ 13.00 ____
CALL TO LOVE............................. 7.00 ____

DEMELLO AUDIOS
A SATELLITE RETREAT................... 23.00 ____
WAKE UP TO LIFE.......................... 59.00 ____

DEMELLO VIDEOS
A WAY TO GOD FOR TODAY............ 43.00 ____
REDISCOVERY OF LIFE .... 43.00 ____
WAKE UP SPIRITUALITY.................. 37.00 ____

DOLAN BOOKS
MEDITATIONS FOR LIFE.................. 12.00 ____
COMMUNION MEDITATIONS........... 6.00 ____
SPIRITUAL EXER. OF ST. IGNATIUS.. 12.00 ____
DINOSAUR SUMMER...................... 8.00 ____

DOLAN AUDIO ALBUMS
COMMUNION MEDITATIONS.......... 18.00 ____
SPIRITUAL AWARENESS................. 18.00 ____
GUIDED MEDITATIONS.................... 18.00 ____
MEDITATIONS FOR LIFE .... 35.00 ____
NOTES ON DEMELLO (VOL. 2).......... 35.00 ____
NOTES ON DEMELLO (VOL. 3).......... 35.00 ____
NOTES ON DEMELLO (VOL. 4).......... 35.00 ____

OTHER AUDIO TAPES
NEW WINE – IS YOUR GOD SMALL.... 10.00 ____

SUBTOTAL $ ____
P& H $ 5.00
TOTAL $ ____

taught you by their behaviour and their panic reactions, that every time the outside world did not conform to a certain pattern, you must create an emotional turmoil within yourself called insecurity.

> And you had to do everything in your power to rearrange the outside world: Make more money, seek more reassurances, placate and please the people you have offended, etc., etc; in order to make the insecurity feelings go away. The mere realization that you don't have to do this, that doing this really solves nothing, and that the emotional turmoil is caused solely by you and your culture, this realization alone distances you from the problem and brings considerable relief.

IV. *Fourth,* whenever you are insecure about what may happen in the future, just remember this: In the past six months or one year you were so insecure about events which when, they finally came you were able to handle somehow.

> Thanks to the energy and the resources that that particular present moment gave you, and not to all the previous worrying which only made you suffer needlessly and weakened you emotionally. So, say to yourself: "If there is anything I can do about the future, right now, I shall do it. Then I'm going to just leave it alone and settle down to enjoy the present moment, because all the experience of my life has shown me that I can only cope with things when they are present, not before they occur. And that the present always gives me the resources and the energy I need to deal with them.

The final disappearance of insecurity feelings will only come when you have attained that blessed ability of the birds of the air and the flowers of the field to live fully in the present, one moment at a time. The present moment, no matter how painful is never unbearable.

What is unbearable is what you think is going to happen in five hours or in five days; and those words you keep saying in your head, words like, "This is terrible, this is unbearable, how long is this going to last, and so on." Birds and flowers are blessed above humans in that they have no concept of the future, no words in their heads, and no anxiety about what their fellows think of them. That is why they are such perfect images of the kingdom.

So do not be anxious about tomorrow, tomorrow will look after itself. Each day has troubles enough of its own. Set your mind on God's Kingdom before everything else and all the rest will come to you as well.

MEDITATION 29

FACING LIFE AND DEATH

*He who finds his life will lose it, and he who
loses his life for my sake will find it. Mt. 10, 39*

Has it ever struck you that those who most fear to
die are the ones who most fear to live? That in
running away from death we are running away from
life?

Think of a man living in an attic, a little hole
of a place with no light and little ventilation.
He fears to come down the stairs because he
has heard of people falling downstairs and
breaking their necks. He would never cross a
street because he has heard of thousands who
have been run over on the streets. And of
course, if he cannot cross a street, how will he
cross an ocean or a continent or one world of
ideas to another. This man clings to his hole
of an attic in the attempt to ward off death
and in doing so he has simultaneously warded
off life.

What is death? A loss, a disappearance, a letting go,
a saying goodbye. When you cling you refuse to let
go, you refuse to say goodbye, you resist death. And

even though you may not realize it, that is when you resist life too.

For life is on the move and you are stuck, life flows and you have become stagnant, life is flexible and free and you are rigid and frozen. Life carries all things away, and you crave for stability and permanence.

So you fear life and you fear death because you cling.

When you cling to nothing, when you have no fear of losing anything, then you are free to flow like the mountain stream that is always fresh and sparkling and alive.

There are people who cannot bear the thought of losing a relative or a friend, they prefer not to think of it; or they dread to challenge and lose a pet theory or ideology or belief; or they are convinced that they are never able to live without this or that precious person, place or thing.

Do you want a way to measure the degree of your rigidity and your deadness? Observe the amount of pain you experience when you lose a cherished idea or person or thing. The pain and the grief betray your clinging, do they not? Why is it you grieve so much at the death of a loved one or the loss of a friend? You never took the time to seriously consider that all things change and pass away and die.

So death and loss and separation take you by surprise. You choose to live in a little attic of your illusion pretending that things will never change, that things will always be the same. That is why when life bursts in to shatter your illusion you experience so much pain.

In order to live you must look reality in the face and then you will shed your fear of losing people and develop a taste for newness and change and uncertainty. You will shed your fear of losing the known and expectantly wait and welcome the unfamiliar and the unknown.

If it is life you seek, then here is an exercise that might prove painful but will bring the exhilaration of freedom if you are able to do it.

I.   Ask yourself if there is anything or anyone whose loss would cause you grief. You may be one of those persons who cannot bear to even think of the death or the loss of a parent, a friend, a loved one. If this is so, and in the measure that this is so, you are dead. The thing to do is to face the death, the loss, the separation, from loved things and loved ones now.

II. Take these persons and things one at a time and imagine they are dead or lost or separated from you forever, and in your heart say goodbye. To each of them say thank you and goodbye.

III. You will experience pain and you will experience the disappearance of clinging; and then something else will emerge in your consciousness, an aloneness, a solitude, that grows and grows and becomes like the infinite vastness of the sky. In that aloneness is freedom. In that solitude is life.

In that non-clinging is the willingness to flow and to enjoy and to taste and to relish each new moment of life which is now made all the sweeter because it is freed from the anxiety and tension and insecurity, freed from the fear of loss and death that always accompanies the desire for permanence and clinging.

MEDITATION 30

CLEAR THINKING, CLEAN HEART

*Your eye is the lamp of your body; when your eye
is sound, your whole body is full of light ; but
when it is not sound, your body is full of
darkness.*   Lk. 11, 34

We think the world would be saved if only we could generate larger quantities of goodwill and tolerance. That's false.

What will save the world is not goodwill and tolerance but clear thinking. Of what use is it to be tolerant of others if you are convinced that you are right and everyone who disagrees with you is wrong? That isn't tolerance but condescension. That leads not to union of hearts but to division, because you are one-up and the others one-down. A position that can only lead to a sense of superiority on your part and resentment on your neighbour's thereby breeding further intolerance.

True tolerance only arises from a keen awareness of the abysmal ignorance of everyone as far as truth is concerned. For truth is essentially mystery.

The mind can sense but cannot grasp it,

much less formulate it. Our beliefs can point to it but cannot put it into words. In spite of this, people talk glowingly about the value of dialogue, which at worst is a camouflaged attempt to convince the other person of the rightness of your position, and at best will prevent you from becoming a frog in the well who thinks that his well is the only world there is.

What happens when frogs from different wells assemble to dialogue about their convictions and experiences? Their horizons widen to include the existence of wells other than their own. But they still have no suspicion of the existence of the ocean of truth that cannot he confined within the walls of conceptual wells. And our poor frogs continue to be divided and to speak in terms of yours and mine, your experience, your convictions, your ideology and mine. The sharing of formulas does not enrich the sharers, for formulas like the walls of wells divide; only the unrestricted ocean unites.

But to arrive at this ocean of truth that is unbounded by formulas, it is essential to have the gift of clear thinking.

What is clear thinking and how does one arrive at it?

I.   The first thing you must know is that it does not call for any great learning. It is so simple as to be within the reach of a ten-year-old child. What is needed is not learning but unlearning, not talent but courage.

> You will understand this if you think of a little child in the arms of an old, disfigured housemaid. The child is too young to have picked up the prejudices of its elders. So when it snuggles in that woman's arms, it is

responding not to labels in its head; labels like white woman, black woman, ugly, pretty, old, young, mother, servant maid, it is responding not to labels such as these but to reality. That woman meets the child's need for love and that is the reality the child responds to, not the woman's name and figure and religion and race and sect. Those are totally and absolutely irrelevant.

The child has as yet no beliefs and no prejudices. This is the environment within which clear thinking can occur. And to achieve it, one must drop everything one has learnt and achieve the mind of the child that is innocent of past experiences and programming which so cloud our way of looking at reality.

II. Look into yourself and examine your reactions to persons and situations, and you will be appalled to discover the prejudiced thinking behind your reactions. It is almost never the concrete reality of this person or thing that you are responding to. You are responding to principles, ideologies, belief-systems, economic, political, religious, psychological belief-systems; to preconceived ideas and prejudices, whether positive or negative.

III. Take them one at a time, each person and thing and situation, and search for your bias, separating the reality here before you from your programmed perceptions and your projections. And this exercise will afford you a revelation as divine as any that the scriptures could provide you with.

Prejudices and beliefs are not the only enemies of clear thinking.

There is another pair of enemies called desire and fear. Thinking that is uncontaminated by emotion, namely by desire and fear, and self-interest, calls for an asceticism that is terrifying.

People mistakenly assume that their thinking is done by their head; it is done actually by the heart which first dictates the conclusion, then commands the head to provide the reasoning that will defend it. So here is another source of divine revelation. Examine some of the conclusions that you have arrived at and see how they are adulterated by self-interest. This is true of every conclusion, unless you hold it provisionally. Think how tightly you hold onto your conclusions regarding people, for instance. Are those judgments completely free of emotion? If you think they are, you have probably not looked hard enough.

> This is the major cause of disagreements and division between nations and individuals. Your interests do not coincide with mine, so your thinking and your conclusions do not agree with mine.

> How many people do you know whose thinking is at least some-times opposed to their self-interest? How many times can you recall having engaged in that kind of thinking yourself? How often have you succeeded in placing an impenetrable barrier between the thinking going on in your head and the fears and desires that agitate your heart? Each time you attempt that task, you will understand that what clear thinking calls for is not intelligence. That is easily come by — but the courage that has successfully coped with fear and with desire, for the moment you desire something or fear something, your heart will consciously or unconsciously get in the way of your thinking.

This is a consideration for spiritual giants who have come to realise that in order to find truth they need, not doctrinal formulations, but:

A. A heart that divests itself of its programming and its self-interest each time that thinking is in progress;

B.   A heart that has nothing to protect and nothing to ambition and therefore leaves the mind to roam unfettered, fearless and free, in search of truth;

C.   A heart that is ever ready to accept new evidence and to change its views.

Such a heart then becomes a lamp that enlightens the darkness of the whole body of humanity. If all human beings were fitted with such hearts, people would no longer think of themselves as Communists or Capitalists, as Christians or Muslims or Buddhists. The very clarity of their thinking would show them that all thinking, all concepts, all beliefs are lamps full of darkness, signs of their ignorance. And in that realization the walls of their separate wells would collapse and they would be invaded by the ocean that unites all peoples in the truth.

MEDITATION 31

DIVINITY IS ALL AROUND YOU

Therefore you also must be ready; for the Son of Man is coming at an hour you do not expect.   Mt. 24, 44

Sooner or later there arises in every human heart the desire for holiness, spirituality, God, call it what you will.

One hears mystics speak of a divinity all around them that is within our grasp, that would make our lives meaningful and beautiful and rich, if we could only discover it.

People have some sort of a vague idea as to what this thing is. They read books and consult Gurus, in the attempt to find out what it is that they must do to gain this elusive thing called Holiness or Spirituality.

People pick up all sorts of methods, techniques, spiritual exercises, formulas; then after years of fruitless striving, they become discouraged and confused and wonder what went wrong. Mostly they blame themselves.

If they had practised their techniques more

regularly, if they had been more fervent or more generous, they might have made it. But made what? They have no clear idea as to what exactly this holiness that they seek is, but they certainly know that their lives are still in a mess, they still become anxious and insecure and fearful, resentful and unforgiving, grasping and ambitious and manipulative of people. So once again they throw themselves with renewed vigour into effort and labour that they think they need to attain their goal.

They have never stopped to consider this simple fact. Their efforts are going to get them nowhere.

Their efforts will only make things worse, as things become worse when you use fire to put out fire.

Effort does not lead to growth; effort, whatever the form it may take, whether it be will power or habit or a technique or a spiritual exercise, does not lead to change.

At best it leads to repression and a covering over of the root disease.

Effort may change the behaviour but it does not change the person.

Just think what kind of a mentality it betrays when you ask, "What must I do to get holiness?" Isn't it like asking, "How much money must I spend to buy something? What sacrifice must I make?" What discipline must I undertake? What meditation must I practice in order to get it? Think of a man who wants to win the love of a woman and attempts to improve his appearance or build his body or change his behaviour and practice techniques to charm her.

You truly win the love of others not by the practice of techniques but by being a certain kind of person. And that is never achieved through effort and techniques. And so it is with Spirituality and Holiness. Not what you do is what brings it to you.

This is not a commodity that one can buy or a prize that one can win. What matters is what you are, what you become.

Holiness is not an achievement, it is a Grace. A Grace called Awareness, a grace called Looking, observing, understanding:

A.   If you would only switch on the light of awareness and observe yourself and everything around you throughout the day,

B.   If you would see yourself reflected in the mirror of awareness the way you see your face reflected in a looking glass, that is, accurately, clearly, exactly as it is without the slightest distortion or addition,

C.   If you observed this reflection without any judgment or condemnation, you would experience all sorts of marvellous changes coming about in you.

> Only you will not be in control of those changes, or be able to plan them in advance, or decide how and when they are to take place.

It is this non-judgmental awareness alone that heals and changes and makes one grow. But in its own way and at its own time.

What specifically are you to be aware of?

1.   Your reactions and your relationships. Each time you are in the presence of a person, any person, or with nature or with any particular situation, you have all sorts of reactions, positive and negative.

2.   Study those reactions, observe what exactly they are

and where they come from, without any sermonizing or guilt or even any desire, much less effort to change them. That is all that one needs for holiness to arise.

But isn't awareness itself an effort?

Not if you have tasted it even once. For then you will understand that awareness is a delight, the delight of a little child moving out in wonder to discover the world. For even when awareness uncovers unpleasant things in you, it always brings liberation and joy. Then you will know that the unaware life is not worth living, it is too full of darkness and pain.

> If at first there is a sluggishness in practising awareness, don't force yourself. That would be an effort again. Just be aware of your sluggishness without any judgment or condemnation. You will then understand that awareness involves as much effort as a lover makes to go to his beloved, or a hungry man makes to eat his food, or a mountaineer to get to the top of his beloved mountain; so much energy expended, so much hardship even, but it isn't effort, it's fun! In other words, awareness is an effortless activity.

Will awareness bring you the holiness you so desire? Yes and no. The fact is you will never know. For true holiness, the type that is not achieved through techniques and efforts and repression, true holiness is completely unself-conscious. You wouldn't have the slightest awareness of its existence in you. Besides you will not care, for even the ambition to be holy will have dropped as you live from moment to moment a life made full and happy and transparent through awareness. It is enough for you to be watchful and awake. For in this state your eyes will see the Saviour. Nothing else, but absolutely nothing else. not security, not love, not belonging, not beauty, not power, not holiness—nothing else will matter any more.

Made in the USA
Monee, IL
24 October 2020

45999881R00163